NEW ENGLAND REMEMBERS

# The Boston Tea Party

## Robert J. Allison

*Robert J. Allison, Series Editor*

*Commonwealth Editions*
*Beverly, Massachusetts*

*For my mother*

Copyright © 2007 by Commonwealth Editions.

ISBN 978-1-933212-11-1

**Library of Congress Cataloging-in-Publication Data**
Allison, Robert J.
  The Boston Tea Party / Robert J. Allison.
    p. cm.—(New England Remembers series)
  Includes bibliographical references and index.
  ISBN-13: 978-1-933212-11-1 (alk paper)
  1. Boston Tea Party, 1773. 2. United States—History—Revolution, 1775–1783—Causes. I. Title.
  E215.7.A44 2007
  973.3'115—dc22                    2007014930

Cover and interior design by Laura McFadden Design, Inc.

Printed in the United States of America

Commonwealth Editions is an imprint of Memoirs Unlimited, Inc., 266 Cabot Street, Beverly, Massachusetts 01915.
Visit us on the Web at www.commonwealtheditions.com.

Front and back cover illustrations: Library of Congress

The New England Remembers series logo features a photo of the Thomas Pickton House, Beverly, Massachusetts, used courtesy of the Beverly Historical Society.

10 9 8 7 6 5 4 3 2 1

# CONTENTS

# FOREWORD

On December 16, 1773, men dressed as Indians boarded three ships anchored in Boston Harbor. Working quickly and efficiently, they brought up from the holds 342 chests containing 92,586 pounds of tea, valued at £9,659 (approximately $1,738,500 today), and dumped the contents overboard into Boston Harbor.

They called it the Destruction of the Tea; Governor Thomas Hutchinson called it high treason. The tea belonged to the East India Company; it had been sent under the direction of the British prime minister, Lord North, who had given the company a monopoly on all tea sold in North America. By destroying the tea, the disguised Bostonians made clear they would not be subject to the rule of North or Parliament.

The British government responded by shutting down Boston's port, suspending the Massachusetts government, and sending military force to govern the rebellious colonists. The Bostonians had decided not to receive the tea; they would have to decide if they would submit or resist.

John Adams called the destruction of the tea "the most magnificent Movement of all," so bold, daring, and unexpected it would be "an Epocha in History." He was right. One of the greatest acts of protest in history, it provoked a reaction from Parliament and galvanized a national cause. Though the participants called it the Destruction of the Tea, New England remembers it as the Boston Tea Party.

*Robert J. Allison, Series Editor*
*Boston, Massachusetts*

# CHRONOLOGY

**1770**

JANUARY
Boston merchants agree to abstain from use of tea until Townshend duties repealed.

**1773**

MAY 10
Parliament passes Tea Act.

SEPTEMBER 6
First publication of Tea Act in America, in New York.

OCTOBER 7
Alarm no. 1, first anti-tea handbill, is circulated in New York.

OCTOBER 18
Mass meeting in Philadelphia resolves not to allow tea to land.

NOVEMBER 3
Sons of Liberty in Boston demand resignations of tea consignees and attack Richard Clarke's warehouse; Clarke and other consignees refuse to resign.

NOVEMBER 5
Boston Town Meeting calls for resignation of tea consignees.

NOVEMBER 17
Boston mob attacks home of tea consignee Richard Clarke.

NOVEMBER 18
Boston Town Meeting calls for consignees to resign; consignees refuse.

NOVEMBER 19
Boston tea consignees ask governor and council for protection; council stalls.

NOVEMBER 23
Committees of correspondence from towns around Boston call for resistance to East India tea.

NOVEMBER 26

Town Meeting in Cambridge adopts Philadelphia resolutions.

NOVEMBER 28

*Dartmouth* sails into Boston Harbor, carrying 114 chests of tea.

NOVEMBER 29

More than 1,000 people attend meeting of "Body of People" in
Boston's Faneuil Hall; crowd has to move to Old South Meeting
House, where more than 2,500 attend; Town Meeting appoints guards
for *Dartmouth*. Governor's Council refuses to aid tea consignees.

NOVEMBER 30

Meeting at Old South rejects Governor Hutchinson's order to
disperse. Mass meeting in Dorchester endorses actions of Boston.

DECEMBER 1

Tea consignees in New York resign, ask Governor William Tryon
to take tea under his protection.

DECEMBER 2

*London* arrives in Charleston, South Carolina, with 257 chests of tea;
*Eleanor* reaches Boston with 114 chests of tea.

DECEMBER 3

Mass meeting in Charleston, South Carolina, forces tea consignees
to resign.

DECEMBER 4

Town Meeting in Charlestown, Massachusetts, adopts Philadelphia
resolutions.

DECEMBER 7

*Beaver,* carrying 112 chests of tea, enters Boston; smallpox reported
on board.

DECEMBER 16

Mass meeting in Boston at Old South; destruction of the tea at
Griffin's Wharf.

DECEMBER 17

Mass meeting in New York resolves against landing tea.

DECEMBER 21

Paul Revere arrives in New York with news of destruction of tea.

DECEMBER 22

Charleston, South Carolina, tea taken ashore and stored in custom-house. *Hayley* sails from Boston for London, carrying news of destruction of tea.

DECEMBER 24

News of Boston's destruction of tea reaches Philadelphia.

DECEMBER 25

*Polly,* with 698 chests of tea, anchors in Chester, Pennsylvania.

DECEMBER 26

About 8,000 people attend meeting in Philadelphia to demand return of tea to England.

DECEMBER 28

*Polly* sails from Delaware River, still carrying its full cargo of tea.

## 1774

JANUARY 9

*Dartmouth* sails for England; Francis Rotch goes with it.

MARCH 6

Brig *Fortune* arrives in Boston from London, carrying tea.

MARCH 8

Tea on *Fortune* is destroyed.

APRIL 18

Tea ship *Nancy,* battered by storms, finally reaches New York.

APRIL 25

*Nancy* departs from New York without unloading tea.

MAY

Tea is destroyed in Annapolis and Chestertown, Maryland.

MAY 10

Bostonians learn that Parliament has closed port of Boston, effective June 1

MAY 17

General Thomas Gage assumes position as governor of Massachusetts.

MAY 31

Governor Thomas Hutchinson leaves Boston.

JUNE 1
Port of Boston is closed.

JUNE 2
Bostonians learn that their government is suspended.

SEPTEMBER
Continental Congress meets in Philadelphia; Suffolk County convention meets in Milton, calls on towns of Massachusetts to continue operating as government and calls for a provincial assembly to govern the province.

OCTOBER 25
Women in Edenton, North Carolina, pledge not to use any tea.

**1873**
DECEMBER 16
At Faneuil Hall celebration of anniversary of Tea Party, Ralph Waldo Emerson reads poem "Boston."

**1955**
Richard "Lord" Buckley, musical hipster, records "Boston Tea Party."

**1967**
JANUARY 20
Boston Tea Party Rock Club opens in Boston, showcase for rock and roll.

**1973**
Boston Tea Party Museum opens, with a Danish brig built in 1908 renamed the *Beaver.*

**2001**
Lightning strikes and destroys Tea Party Museum; *Beaver* taken to Gloucester to be refitted.

**2008**
Boston Tea Party Museum reopens with refit *Beaver* and a 1930s fishing boat remade as the *Eleanor.*

# CHAPTER ONE

# Tea and Politics

PARLIAMENT DID NOT INTEND for the Tea Act to provoke a rebellion in North America. Parliament's discussions in the spring of 1773 barely noted the effect the act might have there. Parliament had spent much of the previous year discussing the problems of the East India Company, one of the largest corporations in the British Empire. The Tea Act of May 1773 was part of an overall strategy to reform the company, giving the British government more of a role in its management and ensuring that some of its revenues directly benefited the empire's coffers.

The East India Company traced its origin to 1603, when Parliament granted a group of merchants, the London East India Company, a monopoly on British trade to India and East Asia. Created at the same time as other corporate ventures that would colonize the New World, the London East India Company had done well in India. In the 1690s its Fort St. George in Bengal had combined with several villages to become the city of Calcutta. Tempted by the profits being made in the India trade, Parliament in 1690 created a rival company, the English East India Company. But the competition hurt both, and it gave French, Dutch, and Portuguese merchants opportunities to gain a greater share of the wealth of the Indies. In 1709 the two companies were combined into the "United Company of Merchants trading to the East Indies," or the East India Company.

The company flourished. Trade produced the company's wealth, and by the 1760s tea from China accounted for 90 percent of the company's profits. Tea had become China's national beverage after 700 A.D., when it was introduced from Southeast Asia, but Europe's beverage of choice remained coffee, imported by Portuguese and Dutch merchants from East Africa. Arab merchants monopolized the trade of Chinese tea, or *chah,* into the Middle East and Russia, bringing it along the Silk Road by the eighth or ninth century. The Dutch opened a trade with Chinese tea merchants in Batavia (now Jakarta) in 1610, and the English gradually developed a taste for tea. By the end of the seventeenth century, the English East India Company was bringing a hundred thousand pounds of tea directly from Canton to England every year. Thirty years later the East India Company exported over a million pounds of tea from China annually, and by the 1760s the East India Company sold four million pounds of tea in England per year. Tea had caught on with the British public. By the 1770s the English were buying enough tea for every man, woman, and child in the kingdom to drink three hundred cups each year.

Though the East India Company did very well with the tea trade, it also paid for the privilege. Parliament taxed the company's tea, with the result that the price to consumers nearly doubled. Buying tea in Canton for one shilling a pound, the company sold the tea in England for more than four shillings a pound, but about two shillings went to the tax collectors. Still, the company doubled what it paid for the tea; but the smugglers bringing tea in from Amsterdam or France, who did not have to pay two shillings in taxes on every pound, could sell their tea in England for half what the East India Company charged. Of the thirteen million pounds of tea being sold in England every year, nearly half had been smuggled.

Tea drinking did not catch on so quickly in the American colonies. The habit had developed first among the wealthier people, among the merchants of Boston, New York, and Philadelphia, and the planters of Virginia and South Carolina. By the 1760s Americans were consuming about one million pounds of tea every year, or an average of 120 cups per person. Tea had become the fifth most important English export to the American colonies, behind cotton and woolen cloth, linen, and ironware. Americans imported mainly the least expensive grade of tea, bohea, as they had not developed a taste for the finer hyson or souchong grades. Not as selective tea connoisseurs as the English, Americans were better smugglers. Smugglers supplied half of England's tea, but they were the source of 90 percent of the tea Americans sipped.

Although the Tea Act of 1773 would give the company a monopoly on all tea sold in the American colonies, Parliament did not pass the act to address the problem of smuggled tea. Frederick, Lord North, the prime minister, pushed the Tea Act to get more control over the East India Company, not the American colonies. The East India Company was on the verge of bankruptcy. India was in the grip of famine, caused by drought. The company's policy of taxing India and using Indian resources to buy Chinese tea was hurting India's people and economy. The drought and famine were limiting the company's revenues, which it hoped to restore by buying Chinese tea.

Lord North agreed to loan the company £1.5 million (approximately $270 million today). In return, he would have the power to appoint councilors to govern the company in India. For North, the American tea market meant very little, but control of the East India Company meant a great deal.

Tea had already become an article of contention between the colonies and England. In 1767 Parliament had imposed taxes on most of the goods the colonies imported. The Americans protested and boycotted British imports. A Pennsylvanian, John Dickinson, clearly set out the reasons for the protests in a series of essays called *Letters from a Farmer in Pennsylvania,* arguing that Parliament could regulate the empire's trade, but it could not tax the colonists. English subjects could be taxed only by their own consent, and the provincial assemblies, chosen by the people of the colonies, had the sole power to tax them. Parliament did not accept this argument, but it became an article of faith among the colonists. Parliament had relented in 1770, rescinding most of the taxes. But Parliament held to the principle that it did have the right and power to tax the Americans, and so to prove this point, Parliament maintained the tax on tea.

American leaders tried to maintain their boycott of English tea. Another essayist trying to wean Americans of the tea habit published a "Sermon on Tea," warning that tea stood for *tatling,* or gossiping; *extravagance;* and *absurdity.* He reported the gossip (tatling) heard around the tea table—Miss S., soon to be married, was reported to be pregnant, and it was suggested that her mother had been "frightened by a mulatto," and on and on, until "the reputations of twenty different persons were wantonly *murdered,* in quick succession, in [the] course of this evening's repast." As for extravagance, the author reported that the tea ceremony robbed people of time and money, and he asked why tea was preferred to herbs grown in American gardens.

And, finally, absurdity: "*Weak nerves* are occasioned by *strong tea.*" In the century since tea had been introduced in Europe, people had lost "some inches of their stature, many degrees of their strength, and disorders have assumed a new complexion." Nervous complaints were increasing, physicians could not cope with new diseases, and the human frame was generally "debilitated." A hundred years earlier, nervous disorders—"Histerica"—had been peculiar to women; now men also suffered. Tea had reduced the "masculine habit of men, to feminine softness. In short, it has turned the men into women, and the women into—God knows what."

The author concluded that tea, like arsenic, was a slow poison that could be introduced gradually into a system. "Tea rendered habitual, gradually saps the constitution, without surprising us with its immediate effects. It is slow but sure."

Tea was slow poison, but it had become a habit among upper-class women. An anonymous poem addressed to the "Tea-Drinking Ladies of New York" in May 1770 lamented:

> *The Ladies are not quite so complaisant,*
> *If they want TEA, they'll storm and rave and rant,*
> *And call their Lordly Husbands Ass and Clown,*
> *The jest of Fools and Sport of all the Town.*

The poet tells how Mr. Hornbloom jubilantly told his wife of the arrival of "noble news" from London—Parliament had repealed most of the import taxes. Madam Hornbloom asks if the ship that brought the news also brought tea, and he tells her,

> *"We can't import that Indian Weed,*
> *That Duty's still a Rod above our Head."*

She orders him back to the ship:

*"Curse on your Heads, you nasty fumbling Crew,"*
*Then round his Shoulders the hard Broom-Stick flew.*

She tells him to bring her some "Shushong," as she had invited Madame Strong to tea.

Madame Strong arrives, apologizes for being late to tea, but her "spraling Brats kept [her] so long at Home," and her "Stupid Husband" had also gone astray—"To wait upon the Sons of Liberty."

FEW AMERICANS WERE THINKING about tea or the problems of the East India Company in 1773. Georgia and South Carolina, both with economies rooted in slave labor, were faced with the power of the Cherokee and Creek people on their frontier. North Carolina was still feeling the aftereffects of a frontier rebellion, sparked by settlers angry at the greed and arrogance of appointed officials. Virginians had cast their eyes across the mountains toward the Ohio River valley—in fact, twenty years earlier their desire to speculate in this interior had led to political strife among Virginia, Pennsylvania, and New York, and conflict between their ambitions and those of the French in Canada sparked a global war between the British and French Empires that had ended, with a decisive British victory, in 1763. Pennsylvania and Connecticut were on the verge of war over land; Connecticut settlers were taking up residence in towns they built in the Wyoming Valley of the upper Susquehanna and sending representatives and paying taxes to the government in Hartford. In New York, landowners and tenant farmers were fighting over rents and taxes, and these disputes spilled over into a conflict between New York and New Hampshire over the Green Mountain territory they both claimed—a conflict that also involved the people in that territory, many of whom preferred to govern themselves.

And, finally, Massachusetts: after the horrible events of March 1770, when British soldiers had shot five people to death in Boston, Massachusetts had been relatively tranquil. The troops had left, and life had gone back to normal. Governor Thomas Hutchinson reported that "if it were not for an Adams or two," he would be doing very well.

Samuel Adams, leader of the Boston Town Meeting and clerk of the Massachusetts Assembly, continued his campaign against the governor; his cousin John, a lawyer, had ably defended the British soldiers who killed the townspeople, but he was even more able in thwarting the governor's authority.

Samuel Adams had the Town Meeting establish the Committee of Correspondence, to communicate with other towns in the province, so that all received news directly from Adams in Boston. In the Massachusetts Assembly he created a similar committee, an official organ of the legislature, to communicate directly with the assemblies of other colonies. This communication network kept like-minded men in each colony in touch with one another.

While relations between each colony and Britain were tranquil, a few issues continued to irritate. The tax on tea was one. Colonial leaders insisted on maintaining a boycott of tea and other British goods, but support for this boycott waned, particularly among some Boston merchants. In fact, the merchants of New York and Philadelphia charged the Bostonians with shirking their common responsibilities to the boycott. Governor Hutchinson, whose sons were merchants, was delighted at the inability of rival Boston merchants to maintain a boycott. The people, he believed, had a right to buy tea or whatever else they chose, and the British Parliament had the power to tax the American colonies.

Hutchinson opened the Massachusetts Assembly's session in 1773 with a long, confident speech, in which he took advantage of this relatively tranquil time to explain to the assemblymen, chosen by the people in the towns of Massachusetts, what their proper role was in the British Empire. They were not a miniature version of Parliament, with sovereign legislative power over the province. They could attend to local matters, but they had to acknowledge that Parliament was supreme in the British Empire. Otherwise, if the Massachusetts Assembly had the sole power to make laws in Massachusetts, then Massachusetts would be independent.

Hutchinson also believed that having the provincial assembly meet in Boston put its members too much under the influence of Boston's political clique, led by Samuel Adams, and made them vulnerable to the Boston Sons of Liberty and other intimidating groups. He suggested that the assembly move to Cambridge, though he had long quietly advocated a move even farther, to Salem. At any rate, Hutchinson informed the assembly, it was his prerogative as governor to tell them when and where they would meet. Their choice in all of this was simple. To submit to the power of Parliament and their governor, or to announce their independence, with all its frightful consequences.

A scholarly and patient man, Hutchinson spent hours lecturing the members of the assembly on their duties and their role in the empire. But the assembly, instead of being taught, rejected Hutchinson's lesson. The assembly's charter gave its members the power to decide when and where they would convene; and as for the choice between submission and independence—they really had no choice. They had never mentioned independence, but they knew submission was impossible.

The Massachusetts Assembly unanimously rejected both Hutchinson's proposal that they move and the very idea that he had any say in the matter. Even members inclined to support Hutchinson could not concede power to him—and they began a campaign to have him removed as governor. Just four years earlier they had forced out Governor Francis Bernard, and they were confident they could do the same thing. They applied to their London agent, Benjamin Franklin, to begin the process of recalling Hutchinson.

While Franklin was beginning this process in England, he came across a cache of letters that Hutchinson, Lieutenant Governor Andrew Oliver, and others in New England had written to Thomas Whately, the secretary to the chancellor of the exchequer, in the wake of the Stamp Act riots of 1765. Whately had written to these Americans to learn why the opposition was so intense to the Stamp Act and to the Townshend duties of 1767, which taxed goods imported into the American colonies. Grateful to have a high-ranking British official soliciting their thoughts, and eager to show that not all Americans were disloyal or rebellious, Hutchinson and the others had unburdened themselves, writing frankly about their own feelings toward the opposition. Hutchinson and Oliver had good reason to dislike their opponents— the Sons of Liberty in 1765 had demolished Oliver's Long Wharf warehouse and ransacked Hutchinson's North End home. To keep order in Boston, some of the Americans wrote, the British government should send military force. As to the frequent charge that Americans were simply trying to protect their God-given rights as Englishmen, Hutchinson scoffed that they could not expect to enjoy all of these rights if they were not in England. Having removed to America, they might have to have their rights "crusht a bit" in order to remain part of the British empire.

Franklin sent these letters to Samuel Adams under a strict order of secrecy—they were private letters, not intended for publication. Adams had all members of the assembly read the letters, and then as word spread about their contents, he claimed to have received another, identical set that he could publish. On June 16 the assembly published copies of the Hutchinson-Whately correspondence. The publication ruined Thomas Hutchinson. He asked for an opportunity to go to England to plead his own cause before the Privy Council.

This was the state of affairs in Massachusetts as word reached Boston that ships carrying East India Company tea would be arriving in the early fall of 1773.

# CHAPTER TWO

# Preparing for the Tea

RICHARD CLARKE AT AGE SIXTY-TWO was New England's second-largest importer of tea. His son Jonathan, twenty-nine, was in London to buy tea in the early summer of 1773. Jonathan Clarke learned that the Tea Act gave the East India Company a monopoly on tea sold in the American colonies. The company would designate certain colonial merchants to be their agents, who would receive the tea on consignment and handle all of the sales, for which they would receive a commission of 6 percent. Seeing that the family firm could not import tea into America on its own account, Clarke wisely bid on a contract to receive a consignment of the company's tea.

The East India Company also awarded consignment contracts to Governor Thomas Hutchinson's sons, Thomas Jr. and Elisha of Boston, Benjamin Faneuil of Boston, and his partner, Isaac Winslow of Plymouth. New York's tea consignees were of equal prominence: Henry White served on the Governor's Council, Frederick Pigou and Benjamin Booth were longtime London merchants and Pigou had worked for the East India Company in Canton, and Abraham Lott was the New York provincial treasurer. In Philadelphia, the prominent Quaker merchants Thomas and Isaac Wharton received contracts for the tea, as did Abel James and James Drinker and Gilbert Barkley, who stayed in England until the tea sailed. In Charleston, South Carolina, Roger Smith and the firm of Leger and Greenwood were the consignees.

The company found space on seven ships to bring the tea to America. The two largest, the *Nancy* and the *Polly,* were bound for New York and Philadelphia, each taking over a ton of tea. The *London* would sail for Charleston, South Carolina, loaded with over two hundred chests weighing seventy thousand pounds. Four vessels were destined for Boston—the Clarkes' ship *William;* the *Dartmouth,* owned by the Quaker Joseph Rotch of Nantucket; the *Eleanor,* owned by the Boston merchant John Rowe; and the *Beaver,* owned by another Nantucketer. By September the ships were prepared to sail, and by mid-October they were crossing the Atlantic.

Philadelphia's merchants took immediate action when they learned that the *Polly,* carrying 698 chests of tea valued at £21,000 (worth $3.7 million today), was bound for their city. A broadside called on the "Inhabitants of Pennsylvania" to thwart the East India Company's "very dangerous Attempt" to land the tea "in this Land of Liberty." The company was acting "under the Direction of a corrupt and designing Ministry," and the importation of its tea would "speedily and effectually change" the "invaluable Title of American Freemen to that of Slaves." The broadside called for a meeting at the State House on Saturday, October 16, at two o'clock in the afternoon.

Philadelphia became the center of opposition. Broadsides and newspaper columns warned of the tea's impending arrival and the consequences of receiving it. Writing to the "Freemen of Pennsylvania," an anonymous author calling himself "Regulus" warned that the "Day is at length arrived, in which we must determine to live as Freemen—or as Slaves to linger out a miserable existence." Much had already been written about the "Tea Scheme," so much that "no virtuous American can remain doubtful of its diabolical tendency," nor could anyone ignore "the duty he owes his country." Regulus warned of collaborators and those who might "refuse a helping zealous Hand to drive from our Doors the piratical Argonauts" carrying the East Indian tea. They must not allow "this JACK O'LANTERN PROJECT of the Ministry to lead us blindly aside from the direct and safe Path of Virtue and Liberty, into the loathsome and dangerous Bog of Seduction, passive Obedience, Tyranny, and all Wretchedness."

Every American was bound to use "all prudent Means" to prevent the tea's landing, and the consignees were "Duty bound" to refuse it. No man with any pretension to freedom could allow his "Wharf, stores, or Dwelling to be made use of, in . . . securing the ministerial Adventure." Their resistance would force the British government to treat "the Americans, in future, as Men who are worthy of Liberty; as Men who, at all events, are determined to enjoy it." Because they had already successfully resisted Parliament's attempts to govern them, "Our Names, as Americans, stand high enrolled in the List of Fame,—and in consequence of our former virtuous Exertions, LIBERTY and AMERICA are now in the Acceptation of the whole World, concomitant Ideas."

Seven hundred Philadelphians crowded the meeting at the State House. The meeting expressed a "general dissatisfaction" that "our fellow subjects in England should form a measure so directly tending to enforce the Act and again embroil us with our parent state." It was "also considered that the proposed mode of disposing of the tea tended to a monopoly, ever odious in a free country," and "a universal disapprobation showed itself throughout the city." The meeting adopted eight resolutions:

- Disposal of their own property is the inherent right of freemen; that there can be no property in that which another can, of right, take from us without our consent; that the claim of Parliament to tax America is, in other words, a claim of right to lay contributions on us at pleasure.
- That the duty imposed by parliament upon tea landed in America, is a tax on Americans, or levying contributions without their consent.
- That the express purpose for which the tax is levied on the Americans, namely, for the support of government, the administration of justice, and the defence of his Majesty's dominions in America, has a direct tendency to render assemblies useless, and to introduce arbitrary government and slavery.
- That a virtuous and steady opposition to this ministerial plan of governing America is absolutely necessary to preserve even the shadow of liberty, and it is a duty which every free man in America owes to his country, to himself, and to his posterity.
- That the resolution lately come into by the East-India company, to send out their tea to America, subject to the payment of duties on its being landed here, is an open attempt to inforce the minis-

terial plan, and a violent attack upon the liberties of America.
- That it is the duty of every American to oppose this attempt.
- That whosoever shall, directly or indirectly, countenance this attempt, or in any wise aid or abet in unloading, receiving, or vending the tea sent, or to be sent out by the East-India company, while it remains subject to the payment of a duty here, is an enemy to America.
- That a committee be immediately chosen to wait on those gentlemen, who, it is reported, are appointed by the East India company to receive and sell said tea, and request them, from a regard to their own characters, and the peace and good order of this town and province, immediately to resign their appointments.

These eight resolutions became the basis for resistance in every other colony. Meanwhile, in Philadelphia committees called on the consignees, and by early December all had resigned their commissions.

THE BOSTON TEA MERCHANT Richard Clarke was awakened very early on the morning of Tuesday, November 2, by a violent knocking on the front door of his School Street house. Looking out, he saw two men in the moonlit front yard (where Benjamin Franklin's statue now stands). They told him they had a letter for him. Clarke sent his servant to fetch the letter. It informed him that the "Freemen" of the province expected the pleasure of his company at noon on the following day, Wednesday, at the Liberty Tree. There he would be expected "to make a public resignation" of his commission to sell tea. Identical letters were delivered to the Hutchinsons and to Benjamin Faneuil, and anonymous hands posted the notice at almost every corner of Boston.

Clarke, the Hutchinsons, and Faneuil met the next day to prepare their response. One of them visited Ebenezer Russell's print shop on Union Street and had him print up a broadside, "The Tradesmen's Protest against the Proceedings of the Merchants." The broadside, signed by "The True SONS OF LIBERTY," claimed that tradesmen—artisans, mechanics, and small shopkeepers—had been hurt by the non-importation scheme created in reaction to the Townshend duties. Trade had suffered, supplies of British goods had dwindled, and smuggling merchants had raised their prices on imported goods. The broadside urged Boston's tradesmen to "Avoid the Trap. Remember the iniquitous Non-Importation Scheme." The broadside blamed Boston's importers of Dutch and other teas for the trouble, blasting the "illegal and underhanded" way they had called the meeting at the Liberty Tree by putting up their notices in the dark of night. Meetings like this would "create Disorder and Tumult" and subvert "that CONSTITUTIONAL LIBERTY we are contending for." Pledging to "walk uprightly, and to eat, drink, and wear whatever we can honestly procure by our Labour; and to Buy and Sell when and where we please," the authors of the broadside taunted the "Bellowing Patriot" that "his thundering Balls" would "only serve to sooth our Sleep."

Early Wednesday morning the invitation to the Liberty Tree again was posted around town, this time with a warning—"Shew me the Man that dare take this down." At eleven o'clock Boston's church bells began to toll, and the town crier walked the streets announcing the meeting. By noon, waiting at the tree were five hundred people. Though Clarke did not go to the tree, he believed those who gathered were "chiefly . . . of the lowest rank."

"You may well judge that none of us ever entertained the least thoughts of obeying the summons sent us to attend at Liberty Tree," he wrote. They chose instead to "oppose the designs of the mob," and gathered together with their allies in the counting room of Clarke's King Street warehouse.

During the fury over the Stamp Act in 1765, mass gatherings at the Liberty Tree had compelled Andrew Oliver to resign his commission as stamp agent. This would have been a familiar story for the Hutchinsons and the Clarkes. Andrew Oliver, now the lieutenant governor of Massachusetts, was the uncle of Elisha and Thomas Hutchinson Jr., and his wife, Mary, was the sister of Hutchinson's wife, Margaret. And Clarke's sister Mary was married to Oliver's brother Peter, the chief justice of the Superior Court. Mary and Peter Oliver were the grandparents of Elisha Hutchinson's wife, Mary Oliver Watson. The men gathered at the Liberty Tree recalled Oliver's recantation, and they also knew about the close family ties among the Hutchinsons, the Olivers, and the Clarkes. Every year on August 14, the anniversary of the date they had destroyed Oliver's warehouse, the Sons of Liberty gathered to assert their power.

But the consignees in 1773 ignored the Sons of Liberty's call. The crowd moved from the Liberty Tree to the Clarkes' warehouse on King Street. William Molineux and Joseph Warren led a delegation of nine men into the warehouse, where they found the Clarkes and their supporters, a total of twenty men, in the counting room. Molineux told Clarke that he and his cohort "had committed a high insult on the people" by ignoring their summons. Molineux then read a statement he had written for Clarke and the other consignees to sign, by which they would resign their commissions and pledge to return the East India tea to England without paying any taxes on it. Unlike the Philadelphia merchants, the Boston consignees refused to sign.

Molineux warned them that by refusing these "most reasonable demands," the consignees could expect to feel "the utmost weight of the people's resentment." The delegation left, and the crowd outside seemed to move off, but it then quickly swarmed back to Clarke's warehouse. Nathaniel Hatch, a judge from Dorchester, ordered the mob to disperse. The crowd attacked, preventing Hatch from locking the doors. Taking the warehouse's outer door off its hinges, the mob rushed into the warehouse and tried to force its way into the counting room. The twenty men barricaded in the counting room prevented the mob from getting in, and much of the crowd dispersed, but enough remained behind to keep the merchants captive for over an hour and a half. When most of the crowd had drifted away, the Clarkes and their allies made their way out of the warehouse. Together they walked up King Street encountering no problem other than "some insulting behavior from a few despicable persons."

The next night they received another threatening letter, this one signed "O.C.": "We do not wonder in the least that your apprehensions are terrible, when the most enlightened humane & conscientious community on the earth view you in the light of tigers or mad dogs, whom the public safety obliges them to destroy." Although the missive went on to say that Bostonians opposed "the idea of spilling human blood," they had recently put to death a petty thief. How much more harshly should they deal with men plotting a "robbery of every inhabitant of this country"? Laws "in the Book of God and nature" called for cutting off such "troublers of the whole congregation." The consignees could not "corrupt, intimidate, nor escape" their enforcers. Their only alternative was "a speedy imitation of your brethren in Philadelphia." Otherwise, their "avarice and insolence" would be given their just rewards. This would be the last warning they could expect "from the insulted, abused, and most indignant vindicators of violated liberty in the Town of Boston."

This intimidation failed. The town leaders called for a regular Town Meeting on Friday, November 5. John Hancock presided over this assembly at Faneuil Hall. Before they got to the issue of the East India tea and the "political plan of the British administration" to destroy their trade and their liberty, the meeting discussed the "Tradesmen's Protest." Someone had seen Customs Commissioner Charles Paxton distributing these fliers on King Street. There were four hundred Boston tradesmen in Faneuil Hall; they were asked to gather on the south side of the hall and find out which of them had made this protest. The four hundred tradesmen unanimously disavowed the "Tradesmen's Protest" and denounced it, its publisher, and its distributors as "false, base and scandalous."

Then the meeting turned to the tea situation. If anyone could show that "the introduction of tea" would not be "detrimental to the interest of the people in general," the meeting asked him to come forward and speak. No one came forward to support the tea. The meeting adopted the Philadelphia resolutions, appointing Hancock, Henderson Inches, Benjamin Austin, Jonathan Mason, and the town's selectmen as delegates to ask the tea consignees for their resignations.

The meeting adjourned so the delegates could call on the merchants. The delegation met with Richard Clarke and Benjamin Faneuil. The Hutchinsons had gone to Milton, and Clarke told the committee he could not speak for all the merchants. He would not be able to have an answer before Monday. The delegation reported back to the Town Meeting, which appointed another committee—Samuel Adams, Molineux, and Warren—to tell Clarke and Faneuil that since they "were not joint factors for the East-India company with the Hutchinsons," but presumably able to "determine for themselves," the Town would expect an immediate answer.

Clarke and Faneuil promised a response in half an hour. Someone in the meeting proposed sending a delegation to Milton to ask the Hutchinsons to resign. The meeting chose Hancock, Samuel Adams, Warren, John Pitts, Samuel Abbot, William Powell, and Nathaniel Appleton.

As the meeting waited for the consignees to respond, Ezekiel Russell, who had printed the "Tradesmen's Protest," tried to save himself from the town's disdain. He did not like being called "false, base and scandalous." He did not necessarily agree with the broadside, but had printed it only for the money. The Town Meeting had not asked Russell for this information, and it dismissed him, as the Town was not interested in "the printer or author of the said paper."

The meeting was growing impatient for Clarke's response. It was on the verge of sending another messenger to Clarke and Faneuil, when an emissary from the merchants, Joshua Winslow, brought in a letter. The letter explained that since the tea had not arrived, and they did not know the terms that the East India Company had put upon it, or how much they would be receiving, "and what obligations of either a moral or pecuniary nature we may be under to fulfil the trust that may be devolved on us," they could not answer the Town. When they knew the circumstances, they would "be better qualified to give a definitive answer to the request of the town."

The meeting immediately and unanimously voted that the answer was not satisfactory. It adjourned until the next morning at eleven o'clock, when it expected to hear the report from the Hutchinsons.

The Town Meeting's committee spent the evening of November 5 tracking the Hutchinsons. At Elisha Hutchinson's Boston home they were told he had gone to Milton, but would be back the next morning. The next morning they called again, but were told he was still at his father's house in Milton with his brother. The committee set off for Milton, but they were told when they arrived at the Hutchinson home that Elisha had indeed spent the night there and had already returned to Boston. When the committee reached Elisha's house in Boston, they were told he had already set out again for Milton.

The committee found Thomas Hutchinson Jr. at home in Boston and read him their resolutions. He promised an answer in a quarter of an hour. He had the letter delivered promptly to the Town Meeting. He knew nothing of the tea, other than that some would be consigned to him. Without more specific knowledge, he could not tell the Town Meeting what he would do. When the tea and his commission to sell it arrived, he would be better informed and better able to answer the Town's questions. The meeting found his reply unsatisfactory. In fact, the replies of all the merchants were "daringly affrontive to the town." It directed the Committee of Correspondence to send the meeting's proceedings to every town in the province.

In Edes and Gill's *Boston Gazette,* a "Poor Old Man," who called himself a "friend to Mr. Clarke and his sons, to the two sons of Mr. Hutchinson, and more especially to Mr. FANEUIL whose generous uncle gave us our hall of liberty," warned his friends "earnestly . . . to yield without delay to their fellow townsmen."

But Clarke and Faneuil, at least, refused to yield. Advised to leave town, and warned that "a number of picked men are determined to break into our house one night this week," Faneuil did not leave his house, but for several hours he hid himself in a closet. Clarke, warned that if he landed his tea he would be torn limb from limb, said that he would indeed be torn limb from limb "before he will desert the Trust reposd in him by the consigners."

Recognizing the potential for a rising tide of violence, Governor Hutchinson called for the Independent Company of Cadets, the Town of Boston's militia force, to be ready to quell disorders. How much faith he would put in this unit is doubtful; John Hancock, who was presiding over the Town Meeting that was protesting the tea's arrival, commanded the company. Perhaps Hutchinson expected that Hancock's loyalty, like his own, would be to the letter of the law; or perhaps he hoped to show Hancock's duplicity. He ordered Hancock to be prepared to aid civil magistrates "in the Preservation of the Peace."

Boston was quiet until Wednesday, November 17, when John Hancock's ship, the *Hayley,* arrived from London. Captain James Scott had refused to carry any of the East India tea, but he did bring home Jonathan Clarke. That night the entire Clarke family, including Richard's son-in-law John Singleton Copley, gathered in Richard Clarke's School Street home.

Suddenly the noise of horns, whistles, shouting, and violent knocking on the door disrupted the party. Ushering the women to the security of the topmost floor, the Clarke men, prepared for violence after the attack at the warehouse, showed their weapons from a second-story window. They saw men outside guarding the alleys to prevent their escape. One of the Clarkes fired a pistol. It is not clear if he hit anyone, but the crowd showered the house with rocks, clubs, and brickbats, smashing

*The tea consignee Richard Clarke, shown here with his daughter's family in London, 1778. His son-in-law John Singleton Copley, who painted the portrait, stands behind him. (Courtesy National Gallery of Art)*

windows and window frames. Aided by reinforcements who made it through the crowd, the Clarkes held off the attackers for two hours.

Knowing this kind of violence would turn public opinion toward the besieged consignees, influential Patriots arrived on the scene to quiet the crowd. An anonymous intermediary promised that if the crowd dispersed, he would see to it that the Clarkes appeared the next day at Town Meeting. Satisfied with this promise, the crowd began to disperse.

But the Clarkes would not agree. "People who were so riotously assembled, and had just committed such a violent Outrage against the Peace of the Community," could not negotiate with the Clarkes. The Clarkes would endure "the most fatal issue" before they made a pact with a mob. The emissary brought this word back to the thinning crowd, but he still persuaded the remaining stragglers to leave.

Resolved not to give in, the Clarkes called on Governor Hutchinson the next day. At the very least they wanted a secure place to unload their tea until the matter was resolved. The town leaders also called for another meeting, perhaps hoping to resolve the issue without more violence. Officially, now that Captain Scott had arrived, the consignees might have received more instructions. They could not plead ignorance as a reason for rejecting the Town's demands.

The town leaders also realized that the violent attacks not only failed to intimidate the Clarkes, but had also made the consignees more sympathetic figures. Boston's reputation for lawlessness and mob violence made it difficult to convince outsiders that Bostonians were on the side of righteousness. But though Clarke and the consignees had the high ground in resisting a mob, would they be justified in resisting the will of the Town?

The Town Meeting assembled on Thursday morning, November 18. It sent a committee to call on the tea consignees. The committee found Clarke and the others gathered at the Province House, the official residence of the governor (between today's Washington and Province Streets), preparing their petition to Governor Hutchinson. Presented with the Town's demands, the consignees promised an answer by three o'clock. The Town Meeting reconvened at three, with John Hancock presiding. Hancock received the consignees' letter, opened it, and read it to the assembly.

Sir,
In answer to the message we have this day received from the town, we beg leave to say we have not yet received orders from the East India Company respecting the expected teas, but we are now further acquainted that our friends in England have entered into Engagements in our behalf, merely of a commercial nature, which puts it out of our power to comply with the request of the town.

Immediately and without discussion, the Town Meeting voted this response unsatisfactory. Just as quickly a motion was made to dissolve the meeting, and with no further discussion, the meeting dissolved. Governor Hutchinson reported that the sudden dissolution of the assembly "struck more terror into the consignees than the most minatory resolves."

What would happen next? With the Town officially handling the response to the tea, the consignees were guaranteed at least the force and protection of the law. But with the Town Meeting dissolved so abruptly, it seemed the Town was leaving the consignees to the mercy of the Sons of Liberty.

Clarke and the consignees reported to Hutchinson and the Governor's Council that they had been "cruelly insulted in their persons and property," that "incendiary letters" had been "left and thrown into their houses in the night," and that Clarke's house had been assaulted by a "tumultuous and riotous assembly of people." Fearing more violence, they asked to turn over their commissions to the governor and the council, requesting them to take on the responsibility of landing and protecting the tea until the consignees could dispose of it, or until they received new instructions from London.

The council met the morning after the Town Meeting. The twenty-eight councilors were chosen every year by the assembly to advise the governor. Hutchinson presided over the Governor's Council, and he could veto appointments to it. (For the previous year he had vetoed the assembly's choice of John Adams.) But the councilors saw their first loyalty to Massachusetts, not to the British Empire. Hutchinson feared that the council "would rather confirm than discourage the people in their irregular proceedings," and his fear was justified. He discussed the "tumults and disorders prevailing in the town of Boston," and he asked the council how to handle the situation. While he was raising this issue, the consignees' petition was brought to the council.

Only eight of the council's twenty-seven members were present. Those present could not agree on a course of action, as some were supporters of the consignees, and others supported the Town. Unable to agree, the council put off a decision until the following Tuesday, November 23. But only seven councilors, a bare quorum, appeared on Tuesday, so the council adjourned until Saturday. It instructed Hutchinson to summon the members who lived within forty miles of Boston. Eleven councilors met on Saturday, debated, and appointed James Bowdoin, Samuel Dexter, and John Winthrop to prepare a report on the debate; they then adjourned until Monday.

As the council was failing to act, the committees of correspondence from the towns of Roxbury, Dorchester, Brookline, Cambridge, Charlestown, and Boston assembled at Faneuil Hall. This committee of committees issued a circular to be sent to every town in Massachusetts. The present situation, the letter began, "engages the attention of all the friends of the happy constitution which our fathers framed and for many years supported with such wisdom and fortitude as rendered them the admiration of the age in which they lived." The committee revered the constitution, by which they meant the government set up under the royal charter of 1691, which gave each town the power to chose representatives to the Massachusetts Assembly, which alone had the power to tax the people of Massachusetts. Now "cruel and relentless enemies" were acting with "open violence" or "wicked artifice" to undermine the constitution. The East India Company's attempt to send the tea was the "master-piece of policy for accomplishing the purpose of enslaving us." The report claimed that the East India Company, suffering because Americans were not buying their tea, had in fact lobbied Parliament to rescind the tea duty. But the wicked ministry had contrived a way of benefiting the company "without repealing their darling act." But by refusing to buy the tea, the Americans would show the company that it could boost its sales in America only by repealing the tea tax.

If Americans accepted the tea, however, they would be accepting Parliament's right to tax them. In a very short time Parliament would lay heavier taxes on every article "which our necessity may require, or our shameful luxury may betray us into the use of." British avarice would never be satisfied until "our own manufactures, and even our land, purchased and cultivated by our hard labouring ancestors, are taxed to support the extravagance and vices of wretches whose vileness ought to banish them from the society of men." The tea was merely the beginning. Like a symptom of plague or pestilence, it was the first telltale sign of illness. But while a plague could destroy only "our mortal bodies," the tea would destroy virtue, far more valuable than life. And the destruction of virtue would lead inexorably to enslavement of Americans.

The *Massachusetts Spy* on November 26 printed a letter sent from England to a Bostonian. "One thing I am certain of," the British nobleman wrote, "that no Governor who follows the instructions of a British ministry will be agreeable on your side of the world, except a very different set of maxims should take place with administration." At the moment, Hutchinson and the Town leaders were both vying for the loyalty of the people of the province; but this British writer believed that loyalty meant "obedience to the laws enacted by ourselves in a body of our representatives." Though the North ministry was trying to

introduce a new system of loyalty, "I will not suffer it to have domin-
ion over me." He concluded his letter with a paragraph received from
"the Great P–TT," William Pitt, the former prime minister: "On the
other side of the Atlantic, we view a world not yet enervated by luxury
nor tainted with corruption; of course, ardent and resolute for LIB-
ERTY. How affecting the spectacle! How does the *Honest Daughter*
shame the *Profligate Mother.*" A Boston correspondent wrote that he
would be less alarmed at a cargo of "the bedding of those unhappy persons" who died of the plague at Baghdad than one consisting of "one
chest of the slave making tea." He warned that "Philadelphia and New
York," which had forced their consignees to resign, "merely shudder in
doubt of our firmness." If Boston deviated "one ace" from the com-
mitment to "destroy, or at best return it, without touching the shore," it
would "so lower us in their esteem" that their confidence never could
be restored. "How fatal this would be to our common liberty, Mr.
Hutchinson, at least knows."

Cambridge's Town Meeting adopted the Philadelphia resolves on
November 26, declaring the consignees enemies to their country and
warning townspeople against sheltering them. Charlestown's Town
Meeting met on November 27, then adjourned until December 4,
when they adopted the Philadelphia resolves.

The problem was still relatively abstract. The tea was coming, but it
had not arrived. All knew it was coming and expected it hourly. The
consignees in Philadelphia and New York, where the bulk of the tea was
going, had already resigned. If the tea reached those ports first, actions
there might influence Boston, where neither the intimidation of the
Sons of Liberty nor the public condemnation by the Town had shaken
the Clarkes, the Hutchinsons, and Faneuil. What would be done when
the tea arrived?

Boston was divided. Philadelphia had taken a clear and decisive
stand and would reject the tea. In New York, though Governor Tryon
pledged to land the tea, the consignees had resigned. But in Boston the
consignees had not been forced to budge. Would Boston receive the
tea? If so, would the other towns be able to resist its landing? If it was
true that the landing of the tea was the first step toward their inevitable
enslavement, then Adams, Molineux, and the leaders of the Sons of
Liberty knew they had to prevent its landing.

# The Tea Arrives

BOSTON WOULD NOT HAVE a precedent to follow. The *Dartmouth,* owned by Joseph Rotch, a Nantucketer then in the whale oil business in the Buzzards Bay port of Dartmouth, sailed into Boston Harbor on Sunday, November 28. It carried 114 chests of tea. At eleven o'clock in the morning it came to anchor about four hundred yards off Long Wharf. Captain James Hall placed the *Dartmouth* just astern of Admiral John Montagu's flagship, *Captain.* Montagu's naval vessel could protect the *Dartmouth* and its cargo of tea.

The 114 chests of tea now having arrived in port, various parties flew into action. William Molineux led a delegation to call on Francis Rotch, son of the *Dartmouth's* owner. Molineaux told Rotch not to enter the ship's cargo in the customhouse register. Boston's selectmen tried to meet with the tea consignees, eager to have them agree to return the cargo. At the very least, the selectmen hoped that they could call a town meeting, which would give a legal channel for opposition, and so possibly prevent violence on the docks.

That afternoon the Committee of Correspondence met and sent messages to committees of the neighboring towns, inviting them to meet the next day at Faneuil Hall. Without waiting for the selectmen to call a town meeting, the committee that night posted a notice around town advertising their gathering:

Friends, Brethren, Countrymen!

That worst of Plagues, the Detestable Tea, ship'd for this Port by the East India Company, is now arrived in this harbour, the Hour of Destruction or manly Opposition to the Machinations of Tyranny stares you in the Face: every Friend to his Country to himself & to Posterity is now called upon to meet at Fanewill Hall at nine of Clock this Day (at which time the Bells will begin to Ring) to make a United & Successful Resistance to this last worst & most Destructive Measure of Administration.

More than one thousand people crowded into Faneuil Hall Monday morning at nine o'clock. Hancock, though chosen, declined to serve as moderator. He explained that he might be needed at the Governor's Council. Jonathan Williams presided. Immediately the motion was made to review the previous Town Meeting's decision to use "the utmost of their Power" to prevent the "landing of the tea." The question was put: "Whether this Body are absolutely determined that the tea now arrived in Capt. Hall shall be returned to the place whence it came?" No one voted against it.

It was clear that Faneuil Hall could not accommodate a crowd this large, so the meeting adjourned to Old South Meeting House, the largest building in town. Before adjourning, the meeting sent another message to the tea consignees, asking if they would now resign their commissions.

Meanwhile, on Saturday, November 27, Hutchinson and the council met at the State House, finally, to consider the consignees' petition. Earlier, the council had appointed a committee to consider the petition. This meeting opened with three members reporting on the tensions in Boston. Their report explained that the relationship between Great Britain and the colonies "has been for some years past very unhappy," since Parliament had been taxing the colonies. The colonies protested that "constitutionally" they had "an exclusive right of taxing themselves," without which "their condition would be little better than slavery."

Each additional tax law, and particularly the Tea Act, increased the conflict. Before Parliament set out to tax the colonies, Boston had "been as free from disturbances as any people whatever." But the Tea Act "in a commercial view, they think introductive of monopolies, and tending to bring on them the extensive evils thence arising." Their "great objection" was that the act was "manifestly intended" to secure payment of the tax duties levied in 1767. These revenues had already caused conflict, notably in Massachusetts with the dispute over judges' salaries. Having the king pay the judges would tend "in all constitutional questions and in many other cases of importance to bias the judges against the subject."

The committee summarized the reasons for the people being so disturbed before turning to the problems of Clarke and the other consignees. It was clear where the committee's sympathies lay. The council advised that rioters should be prosecuted, but it asked if the Clarkes and the others had applied first to the justices of the peace for protection.

The council refused to take the tea off the consignees' hands. The councilors knew that if they did so, they would be liable for any loss on the sale. The council also knew that landing the tea would make it subject to the tax, and to do this would violate "the declared sentiment of both houses" of the General Court against payment of the tax.

The council advised Hutchinson to renew his call for the sheriffs and justices of the peace to "exert themselves to the utmost" in preserving order. Hutchinson was furious. He demanded to know if the council would "give him no advise on the disorders then prevailing in the town of Boston." The councilors replied that they had already done so: they had told him and the consignees that the tea was their problem.

"What am I in duty bound to do?" Hutchinson asked a London correspondent. He thought he should take refuge on Castle Island, as the people of Boston, meeting "under color of law" night after night in Faneuil Hall, were declaring themselves "in a state of nature," invoking their right to take up arms, and allowing rioters to "attack the persons and the property of the king's subjects." Worse, the "infection is industriously spreading and the neighboring towns not only join their committees with the committee of Boston," but also hold town meetings to approve of Boston's conduct.

While the council was meeting in the State House, twenty-five hundred people crowded into Old South. Francis Rotch and Captain James Hall attended, and they were instructed not to record the tea at the customhouse. Rotch protested and said that if he tried to send the tea back to England, the customs authorities there, or even at Castle Island, would seize his vessel. He announced that he would file a protest at the customhouse, charging that because of political turmoil he could not land his cargo. Samuel Adams told Rotch that he was within his rights to protest—under the law, a shipowner could enter a protest at the customhouse that his goods were "lost or destroyed in a storm." Rotch might be "compelled by a Political Storm to return the Tea." He could "safely and honestly" protest that "a Mob of several Thousands" had forced him to return the tea; in fact, it might be necessary "for the Safety of his Person and Property so to do." The meeting advised Rotch that he would land the tea at his peril.

The meeting appointed twenty-five men, led by Captain Edward Proctor, to guard the *Dartmouth*. It called for nightly watches of twenty-five to protect the ship and ensure it did not unload. But before the meeting adjourned, a message came that the governor, heeding the council's call for action, had issued a writ to justices of the peace, advising them to use their powers to suppress riots. Hancock observed that this was one more instance "of the restless Machinations of that Tool of Power and Enemy of his Country," Thomas Hutchinson, trying to find a pretext to bring troops into town. Hancock reported that in the morning's council meeting the governor had tried to get the tea under his protection, but the council had wisely refused either to take the tea or to advise Hutchinson on what to do with it. The assembly declared "that the Governors conduct herein does not reflect greatly upon the People and is solely calculated to serve the views of his administration."

On Tuesday morning, November 30, the Boston Committee of Correspondence ordered Captain Hall to take his ship to Rowe's Wharf, where it would be under their protection, rather than the protection of Admiral Montagu. John Rowe ultimately prevailed on the committee to allow the *Dartmouth* to dock at Griffin's Wharf rather than his own.

With the cargo now under watch, the town still needed to deal with the consignees. John Singleton Copley and a selectman, John Scollay, were both trying to resolve the crisis. Scollay thought that the consignees could put the tea in storage until they received orders from the East India Company, and they then could send it back to England. Copley had told the consignees that they should send "something in writing" to the selectmen to "prevent immediate outrage." The consignees did put something in writing—a letter absolutely refusing to send the tea back to England. Copley wisely decided not to show this letter to the meeting. He persuaded the consignees to write a more conciliatory message, which he presented at the Tuesday gathering.

At that meeting, on November 30, Hancock announced that Copley had told him the consignees had not received their orders from London until the previous evening, after the *Dartmouth* had arrived. They were now too dispersed to meet together and so could not answer the Town. That day, though, they wrote to Scollay, telling him they were sorry they could not send satisfactory answers to the Town's previous two messages. "We still retain a disposition to do all in our power to give satisfaction to the Town," they wrote, but since "nothing less than sending back the teas" would satisfy the Town, and since this was beyond their power, they hoped the Town would be satisfied if the consignees stored the tea "until we shall have an opportunity of writing to our constituents."

Before the Town could respond to the consignees' request for time and patience, Sheriff Greenleaf arrived. Greenleaf, seventy-two years old and having been intimidated in the past by unruly gatherings of Sons of Liberty, had a proclamation from Governor Hutchinson. Either Adams or Hancock moved that Greenleaf read the proclamation.

Hutchinson's proclamation declared the meeting illegal, that it was called "for certain unlawful purposes," in open violation of "the good and wholesome laws of the Province, and the constitution of government under which they live," and he warned and exhorted all in attendance "to disperse and surcease all further unlawful proceedings at your utmost peril." As Greenleaf finished, a "loud and very general hiss" filled the hall. Then Samuel Adams rose and spoke for fifteen or twenty minutes, vilifying the governor and his proclamation, noting how often Hutchinson used the word "unlawful," a word that Adams said insulted the "free and sensible People," who felt themselves injured and "had a Right to meet together to consult for their own Safety." Far from being riotous, "they were as regular and orderly as any People whatsoever," on a par with their House of Representatives or the House of Commons.

Adams had particular words for the beginning and end of Hutchinson's proclamation. Thinking that Hancock would preside over the meeting, the governor had addressed the message to him, but now Hancock's name was crossed out and Jonathan Williams's written in— "another instance of the Governor's implacable Hatred to that worthy and inflexible Patriot," Hancock. In his conclusion, Hutchinson had written of himself "as his Majesty's Representative in the Province," to which Adams exclaimed, "He? He? is he that Shadow of a Man, scarce able to support his withered Carcase or his hoary Head! is he a *Representation of Majesty?*"

Without a dissenting voice, the assembly voted to ignore the governor's order.

The merchant John Rowe, the owner of the wharf and of the ship *Eleanor* bound for Boston with a cargo of tea, was in attendance. He was called up to the front and informed that Rotch would permit the *Dartmouth* to return to England with *its* cargo of tea. Rowe was sorry his ship had any of that "detestable and obnoxious Commodity" aboard, but he was in a quandary. On his wharf he had a full cargo waiting for the *Eleanor* to carry to England; he needed to unload the tea before he sent the *Eleanor* back. He hoped his captain would act with reason, and he apologized again for having the tea aboard. As he spoke the audience warmed to him, and he to them. Thinking about his full ship, his waiting cargo, and the unwanted tea, he asked "Whether a little Salt Water would not do it good, or whether Salt Water would not make as good Tea as fresh."

The hall erupted with shouting and applause, and someone commented "that now they had brought a good Tory over to their Side— that Mr. Rowe had now become a good Man and they should soon make all the rest of the Tories turn to their Side as Mr. Rowe had done."

Copley asked if he could bring the Clarkes to the meeting. He asked if they would "be treated with civility" despite their disagreement with the gathering. It was agreed, and the meeting adjourned until two o'clock. Copley took a boat to Castle Island, where the Clarkes had taken refuge. He convinced them that they would be safe at the Town Meeting, but the Clarkes knew that nothing short of shipping the tea back to England would satisfy the people, and that they could not do. They proposed John Scollay's idea of storing the tea under the Town's supervision. And since they "had not been active in introducing the tea," they would not obstruct the people "in their procedure with the same." But they would not resign. The consignees also noted that other Boston merchants, now allied with the Town in its protests against them, had been importing British tea despite the nonimportation agreement. Why were the consignees now being singled out for public outrage? Copley returned alone to Boston with this message.

Without the consignees, the Town Meeting turned on the other Boston merchants who had been importing British tea, in violation of the nonimportation agreement. The actions of these merchants had particularly offended the merchants of Philadelphia and New York, who had more actively upheld the nonimportation agreement. Recognizing that their own merchants had "justly incurred the displeasure of our Brethren in the other Colonies," the Boston meeting declared that any merchant or captain importing tea was "an enemy to his country." The meeting sent this message to England, and to all the seaports in Massachusetts.

Finishing its work, the meeting appointed Samuel Adams, John Hancock, William Phillips, John Rowe, and Jonathan Williams to prepare a report on the proceedings to be sent to other colonies and to every town in the province. It called on men from other Massachusetts towns to be ready to assist Boston on the first notice of the arrival of more ships, and it thanked these out-of-towners for attending the long days of meetings. Hancock dismissed the assembly, saying, "My Fellow Countrymen, we have now put our Hands to the Plough and Woe be to him that shrinks or looks back."

On December 2 John Rowe's ship *Eleanor* came into Boston with over one hundred more chests of tea; it was ordered to Griffin's Wharf (in the general vicinity of today's Intercontinental Hotel), also to be guarded by twenty-five men at night. The *Beaver* appeared in the harbor on December 7, but smallpox as well as tea was reported on board, so it stayed off Rainsford Island for a week. Reports reached Boston that the fourth ship, the Clarkes' brig *William,* had gone aground off Cape Cod. Jonathan Clarke sailed for Provincetown to take charge, though by the time he reached the Cape most of the tea had disappeared, taken by various Cape Cod beachcombers.

With an impasse at Boston, the committees of correspondence worked to mobilize the rest of the province. The Dorchester meeting on November 30 vowed not to be second to "the bravest of our patriotic

Brethren" in recovering their rights. Dorchester endorsed the "public conduct" of Boston and Cambridge, and it also promised that any "Enemies to this Country" who fled Boston "to shelter themselves from the just Vengeance of their Fellow-Citizens" would be overtaken in Dorchester by the "just indignation" they feared. Though "we are not all of one Town, yet all embarked in one common Cause."

Roxbury, Brookline, Newburyport, Newbury, Lynn, Worcester, Brimfield, Montague, and Plymouth also joined with Boston in publicly opposing the landing of the tea. Roxbury's resolutions blasted the consignees for preferring "their own private emolument to the public Happiness," and for showing "A Temper enemical to the Rights, Liberties, and Prosperity of America." Brookline noted that "Richard Clarke and Son, and Thomas and Elisha Hutchinson, of Boston," had brought themselves "into Contempt" for their refusals to resign. Such "unfeeling Wretches are a Disgrace" for their "sordid Attachment to their private Interest," and they were now "Fugitives from the just Resentment of their affronted Townsmen." Marblehead wished "to be free from the Company of such unworthy Miscreants" as the tea consignees. The people of Plymouth pledged their "lives and fortunes" in defense of their God-given rights, and to use "our whole force" against the "violence and wickedness of our common enemies."

MESSENGERS CARRIED THESE RESOLVES back to Boston, where the newspapers duly printed them. Other messengers carried the Boston resolves to New York and Philadelphia, so that by early December the impression was inescapable that this was a common cause among the North American colonies. On December 2 the ship *London,* with 257 chests of tea, arrived in Charleston, South Carolina. Handbills circulated the next day calling for a meeting of all inhabitants, "particularly the Landholders," on Friday, December 4, at the Great Hall over the Exchange. So many people—landholders and merchants, traditionally in opposite camps—attended the meeting that the Exchange's main beams began to give way. The Charleston tea consignees attended the meeting and resigned their commissions, and the merchants and landholders of South Carolina vowed to refuse any tea until the taxes were repealed.

New York's Sons of Liberty were less successful than the Bostonians in securing unanimous public opinion. They forced the consignees to resign on December 1, but Governor William Tryon made it clear that, consignees or no consignees, he would have the tea landed. Tryon had only recently arrived in New York after a contentious administration in North Carolina, where he had put down a major rebellion by back-country settlers and had embroiled himself in controversy by building a stately governor's palace at New Bern.

Now Tryon promised the consignees he would take the tea under his protection, and James Vardill, writing under the pseudonym "Poplicola," took up the East India Company in a series of essays addressed "To the Worthy Inhabitants of the City of New York." Speaking the language of "Candour and Simplicity," Poplicola said that the opposition's central idea, that "if we purchase the Tea, our Money will be taken from us *without our Consent,* is, I believe, a position too ridiculous to be any longer imposed on the most Credulous." No one was being forced to buy anything. People could decide for themselves to buy or not to buy tea. Poplicola recited the advantages the entire British Empire, including New York, reaped from the East India trade. Having the East India Company strengthen the trade of the empire benefited New York, and New Yorkers who loved their country should support British merchants, rather than the Dutch merchants who were also vying for control of the East Indies. Those New York merchants attacking the East India Company were motivated by self-interest, not patriotism. "While they pretend a zeal for our property, they are pulling down its inclosures. While they cry, a storm is approaching, they through overboard the compass, and break the helm. While they exclaim against tyranny, they are exercising it against our fellow citizens."

Poplicola's arguments touched a nerve. If Poplicola truly was a "great friend to his country," one anonymous writer demanded, he would sign his own name. A writer calling himself "An Old Prophet" blasted Poplicola's "chain of the most impudent falsehoods against their LIBERTIES." "A Student of the Law" called Poplicola "a Disgrace to Human Nature," not courageous enough to be a highway robber, but base enough to pick pockets. Seeing these attacks on him as evidence of the opposition's dishonesty and intellectual bankruptcy, Poplicola printed some of the more extreme examples as footnotes to his essays.

Poplicola even cited John Dickinson's *Letters from a Farmer in Pennsylvania* of 1767, the most important pro-American writing to that date, to support the idea that the Tea Act was a constitutional exercise of Parliamentary power. While denouncing Parliament's attempts to tax Americans, Dickinson had recognized Parliament's power to regulate colonial trade. Dickinson had also disapproved of the Sons of Liberty and their violent Stamp Tax protests, saying that objections should be made in a spirit of "prudence, justice, modesty, bravery, humanity, and magnanimity." Poplicola approvingly quoted Dickinson: "The cause of liberty, is a cause of too much dignity to be sullied by *turbulence* and *tumult.*"

Dickinson himself entered the fray from Pennsylvania with "A Letter from the Country," firmly against the Tea Act. He warned that the East India Company was trying "to repair their broken Fortunes by the Ruin of American Freedom and Liberty!" Were Americans to be "given up to the Disposal of the East India Company," which was allied with Lord North in a plot to enslave America? Dickinson pointed to India as an example of how the company regarded "the Laws of Nations, the Rights, Liberties, or Lives of Men." In India the company "levied War, excited Rebellions, dethroned Princes, and sacrificed Millions for the sake of Gain." It had "reduced whole Provinces of India to Indigence and Ruin." In one year alone, "Fifteen hundred Thousand" people in India died of famine "not because the Earth denied its Fruits," but because the East India Company had "engrossed all the Necessaries of Life, and set them at so high a Rate, that the Poor could not purchase them."

Dickinson warned that tea was but a small part, and a first step of the "Plan they have formed to strip us of our Property." Having drained the fabled wealth of India, the East India Company now "cast their eyes on America, as a new Theatre" for its "talents of Rapine, Oppression, and Cruelty." America would suffer the fate of India if the company was allowed to sell tea. But Dickinson thanked "GOD, we are not Seapoys, nor Marattas," two Indian peoples the company had subjugated, "but British Subjects, born to Liberty, who know its worth, and who prize it high."

He called on Americans to disappoint the company's malice; he knew that "no Man will receive the Tea," no man would rent out warehouse space for the tea, no one would allow a vessel carrying the tea to dock at his wharf, and anyone who did assist in unloading, landing, or storing the tea would be "ever after deemed an Enemy to his Country." Indeed, Dickinson knew that American longshoremen would never lend a hand to unload the tea, as these workers would rather go hungry than "touch the accursed Trash," even for double their wages. All Americans would unite in this cause, Dickinson knew, for "there is a Spirit of Liberty and a Love of their Country among every Class of Men among us," which makes them worthy to be called "free-born Americans."

BACK IN BOSTON, Rotch and Captain Hall visited the consignees at Castle Island. They wanted to know, formally, if the consignees were prepared to receive the tea. They also wanted to be paid the cost of shipping, £97 7s. 7d. (approximately $17,000 in today's currency). The consignees evaded answering the first question, insisting it was out of their power to receive the tea. They also observed that "a number of armed men" had taken control of the ship and, pointing to the printed proceedings of the Town Meeting, that Rotch had already consented to have the tea returned to England. As to the money, the consignees would not pay for the tea until they received it. Three days later Captain Bruce from the *Eleanor* visited Castle Island, and he was also rebuffed. Rotch and Bruce entered protests against the consignees, wanting them to pay for their losses in carrying the tea that the consignees refused to receive.

The consignees would not waver. But among the tea's opponents, cracks were beginning to appear. When Plymouth's Town Meeting reassembled on December 13 to consider laying out a new road, six citizens appeared with a petition signed by forty residents, which protested Plymouth's resolves of the week before. The Plymouth protestors saw no reason for their town to adopt the measures of Philadelphia. Saying they were "neither captivated by sounds and declamations, nor deceived" by the "specious masque of patriotism," these forty individuals called the Boston meetings unlawful and irregular and the personal attacks on the consignees indecent and unjust. The protestors saw "dangerous and fatal consequences" from the town resolves, fearing they would bring down "the vengeance of affronted Majesty" on their town of Plymouth. Calling the protest out of order, the meeting refused to hear it and adjourned.

The protestors were right; resistance to the tea would have dire consequences. But their protest had a more immediate consequence for them. They had publicly identified themselves with the consignees, and with the East India Company, and so they found themselves under attack. By the end of the month, facing intense public pressure, thirteen of the protestors recanted.

On Monday, December 13, the committees of correspondence from the towns around Boston summoned Francis Rotch to a meeting at Faneuil Hall. Why had he not sent the *Dartmouth* back to England? Rotch told them he had made the earlier promise on an unadvised impulse. On reflection, and after consulting counsel, he realized that if he sent the ship back he would be financially ruined. They asked if he would demand a pass for his ship from the customhouse, which would allow him to send the *Dartmouth* to sea without unloading. If the customs officers refused the pass, would he enter a protest? Would he demand another pass and order the *Dartmouth* to sea? No, he would not.

The committee knew time was running out. Under the law, a ship had twenty days from the time it reached port either to unload or to sail away. Once a ship was in port for twenty days, its cargo had to be taxed. The *Dartmouth's* twenty-day grace period would expire on Friday, December 17. By law, the ship then might be forcibly unloaded. The committee posted notices throughout Boston the next morning, Tuesday, December 14: "Friends, Brethren, Countrymen,—The perfidious art of your restless enemies to render ineffectual the late resolutions of the body of the people demand your assembling at the Old South meeting-house, precisely at two o'clock, at which time the bells will ring."

The meeting opened at two. Charlestown's David Cheevers was nominated to preside, but when he could not be found, Samuel Phillips Savage of Weston took the rostrum. Savage's brother Arthur was the deputy surveyor in the customs office; Samuel Savage was from well outside Boston, and so his appointment gave the appearance that this was a provincewide protest. The meeting opened with a reading of the proceedings at Plymouth.

Captain Bruce, of the *Eleanor,* was asked if he would demand a clearance from the customs officers to sail out of the harbor; and even if the customs officers refused, would he sail for London? He told the assembly he would demand a clearance; but knowing that Admiral Montagu's fleet and the guns of Castle Island were prepared to use force against violators of the law, "he was loath to stand the shot of thirty-two pounders."

Rotch was called in and asked why he had not returned the tea to England. Had he not assured the earlier meeting he would do so? Rotch told the assembly that he had consulted with advisors, and he had realized that "if he complied" with the town's demands, "he must be ruined." He did not feel compelled to honor a pledge he had made "thro' Fear." He "would go as far as any reasonable man should say that he ought for the Good of his Country, but he could not see the Justice or Patriotism of his being put in the Front of the Battle."

After all, it was not his fight. He knew that every man in the assembly was aware "of the Impossibility of his getting the Tea back, or that he must be ruined for the attempt." He was willing to bear his share of the loss, but did not see why he—and he alone—should be completely ruined. The East India Company would not be harmed, the Clarkes and the Hutchinsons would not suffer, but he would be destroyed. Rotch offered to have any merchant appraise the ship, so that he could be compensated somehow for it. If "they were determined to destroy the Vessel, he tho't it but just they should bear a Part in the Loss." Rotch would take no further steps toward reshipping the tea under these circumstances, but he "would *Hazard his Life* first."

The Patriot Josiah Quincy rose and said he thought Rotch's proposal made sense. It would be cruel to put Rotch "in the Front of the Battle." Since it was the cause of all Americans, the "People ought to be Sharers" in Rotch's loss. "Humanity was a first Rate Virtue," Quincy said. Patriotism without humanity was not true patriotism. Hoping to spark the assembly to contribute, Quincy pledged "fifty Guineas" toward the purchase and return of the *Dartmouth*. As he finished, a voice from the gallery called out, "You speak Sir very finely, but you don't shew your Money."

Quincy took this as a challenge. The voice implied that Rotch had bribed Quincy to come to his defense, that Rotch had put up the fifty guineas for Quincy to offer so magnanimously. Quincy flatly and angrily denied the charge of bribery, and he called anyone accusing him a scoundrel. Rotch came to Quincy's defense; he said he was surprised that no merchant or even any citizen "had till then shewn the Generosity to espouse his Cause" and offer to share Rotch's suffering.

But the town did not take up the Rotch's cause. Instead, he was told to apply for a pass to clear his ship out of Boston, and the town appointed a committee of ten, including Samuel Adams and Drs. Warren, Thomas Young, and Benjamin Church, to accompany Rotch to the customhouse.

Rotch and the committee called on the customs collector Richard Harrison, who said he could not issue a pass without consulting with the comptroller, Robert Hallowell. He promised a decision the next morning. The committee and Rotch returned to the meeting, which adjourned until Thursday, December 16.

Harrison and Hallowell knew the law. Even though the tea had been in port under twenty days, it had been entered in the customs register, and so technically it did not matter whether the tea was on the *Dartmouth* or on the dock. Under the law, it could not leave Boston; even if it did, it could not legally be reimported into England. On Wednesday morning, Harrison told Rotch he could not issue a pass.

More than five thousand people crowded into Old South Meeting House when the meeting resumed at ten o'clock on Thursday morning. It was a rainy day, and yet even more people crowded the streets outside. Rotch was called in and was informed that he should go to protest at the customhouse, and then apply to Governor Hutchinson for a pass to sail that day to London. The meeting adjourned until three o'clock to give Rotch time to go to Milton and ask Hutchinson for a pass.

At three the meeting resumed. With no sign of Rotch, it heard resolutions from several towns against drinking tea. Boston welcomed these resolutions, and the Town passed its own, describing the use of tea as "improper and pernicious." It called on every town to appoint a committee of inspection to prevent "the detested tea from coming into any of our towns." As the meeting waited impatiently for Rotch, it discussed its former resolution not to let the tea land. Once more it passed the resolve.

At four-thirty, after "sitting upon thorns for an hour and a half," some, who perhaps knew that plans had been made to keep the tea from landing, wanted to dissolve the meeting. Others who had come in from the country did not want to have to go home and come back the next day. News arrived that someone had seen Rotch on the road to Milton; they decided to wait until six. There were more speeches, and the crowd grew eager for action. Josiah Quincy, possibly knowing what was to come that night and sensing what would follow, cautioned moderation.

It is not . . . the spirit that vapors within these walls that must stand us in stead. The exertions of this day will call forth events which will make a very different spirit necessary for our salvation. Whoever supposes that shouts and hosannas will terminate the trials of the day, entertains a childish fancy. We must be grossly ignorant of the importance and value of the prize for which we contend; we must be equally ignorant of the power of those who have combined against us . . . to hope that we shall end this controversy without the sharpest, the sharpest conflicts.

Quincy knew that the events that night would set in motion a violent conflict, worse than the enthusiastic men in the hall could imagine. They flattered themselves, he said, to think that "popular resolves, popular harangues, popular acclamations, and popular vapors will vanquish our foes." Instead of making speeches and passing resolutions, they should "look to the end. Let us weigh and consider before we advance to those measures which must bring on the most trying and terrible struggle this country ever saw."

# CHAPTER FOUR

# The Destruction of the Tea

THE RAIN HAD STOPPED and night had fallen when Rotch returned shortly before six. He had met with Governor Hutchinson. His formal protest was not complete, so he could not show it to the governor, but he told Hutchinson that he had begun the process. According to Hutchinson's account of the meeting, Rotch believed some of the townspeople would be satisfied if the *Dartmouth* sailed away from the dock, and if Admiral Montagu then forced it to stop at Castle Island. There the tea could be stored under the protection of both the cannon and the consignees. Hutchinson liked the idea, but Rotch thought it would be impossible to complete the sailing maneuvers safely. Hutchinson then told him that the *Dartmouth* would be treated no differently from any other ship, that Hutchinson would grant anything "consistent with the laws and his duty to the King," but he could not grant a pass unless the customs officers cleared the ship.

As Rotch finished his account, there was a war whoop in the street, and whistling and yelling, which was answered by a whoop from the gallery. Savage gaveled for silence.

Asked if he would send the tea back, Rotch told the assembly he could not. Asked if he would land the tea, he said "he had no business to do it unless he was called upon by the proper persons, in which case he should attempt to land it for his own security."

Rotch was anxious to get the tea off of his ship.

Samuel Adams rose and said, "This meeting can do nothing more to save the country."

Another war cry outside was answered by another from the gallery, where an apprentice (probably Adam Collson) shouted, "Boston Harbor a teapot tonight! Hurrah for Griffin's Wharf!" Savage pounded his gavel for order, and then Adams suggested that Dr. Young make a speech. The doctor rose and gave a speech on the baneful effects of tea. "He affected to be very merry," telling the audience to refrain from drinking tea and to stand by one another "in Case any should be called to an Account for their Proceedings."

As he spoke, the crowd thinned, and once he was done, Savage gaveled the meeting to a close. But even then, as the crowd dispersed, Adams, Hancock, Warren, and a few other leaders made a point of remaining in the nearly empty Old South. They wanted to be seen in this public place rather than at the scene of the real action.

While the assembly had been waiting impatiently for Rotch's return from Milton, squads of men had gathered in three places: John Crane's carpenter shop on the corner of Hollis and Tremont streets; at the Court Street printing office of Edes and Gill; and at the Green Dragon Tavern on Union and Hanover Streets. Unfortunately, none of these gatherings kept minutes of their meetings or published their resolutions. We know very little about who they were or how they had organized this event. The Green Dragon Tavern was the meeting place of St. Andrews Lodge; their record book simply says that on the evening of December 16 the lodge convened for its weekly meeting, there were not enough members present, and the lodge adjourned. Three members of the lodge— Paul Revere, Samuel Peck, and Thomas Urann—participated in the destruction of the tea.

A similar group gathered in the Long Room above Edes and Gill's shop, where the radical *Boston Gazette* was published. This Long Room was the headquarters of the Long Room Club, whose seventeen members included Hancock, Quincy, and Samuel Adams. These men were conspicuous in their lingering at Old South. The only member of the Long Room Club who participated in the tea's destruction was Paul Revere.

In each of these places men were disguising themselves, smearing their faces with soot, putting feathers in their hair, covering themselves

The Green Dragon.

*The Green Dragon Tavern, where St. Andrews Masonic Lodge met on the night of December 16, 1773. (Courtesy Library of Congress)*

with blankets and arming themselves with pistols and hatchets, preparing for the call to action. The well-known leaders were noticeably absent; instead, according to Joshua Wyeth, a journeyman blacksmith living with his Tory employer, "most of the persons selected for the occasion were apprentices and journeymen," unlikely to be recognized. We do not know, and we probably never will, who organized these three groups or how they conceived their plan. The thirty to fifty core participants, and the fifty or so others who joined in, knew that what they were planning was high treason and that they would be committing it within a few hundred yards of Admiral Montagu's warships.

Just after six o'clock a small group of these disguised Indians reached Old South, whooped as a signal, heard the whoop returned from the galleries, and set off for Griffin's Wharf. Some of the crowd followed, and at Fort Hill the three contingents, from Crane's, the Green Dragon, and Edes and Gill's, joined together. Two by two the men marched to the wharf. By this time the crowd had flooded out of Old South and followed the action down to the docks.

THE ATTACKS ON CLARKE'S SHOP and home had been violent affairs. Some of the men now marching to the wharf had been involved in those brawls. On this moonlit night, though, the men worked calmly and efficiently, taking pains to damage nothing other than the tea. Some among the two thousand spectators commented on the quiet of the night, as the steady noise of axes and hoists was all that was heard. It was a well-organized, well-coordinated effort. Even Admiral Montagu was heard to remark that "these were not a Mob of disorderly Rabble . . . but men of Sense, Coolness, and Intrepidity."

At the dock the parade divided into three groups, each with its own captain, and, joined by apprentices or others from the Old South crowd, boarded the three ships—the *Dartmouth* and *Eleanor* at the dock, the *Beaver* just off the pier. Lendell Pitts, one of the captains, told George Robert Twelves Hewes, a shoemaker, to get the keys, manifest, and a dozen candles from the ship's captain. Hewes did so, and the captain "promptly" complied, asking Hewes "to do no damage to the ship or rigging." The captains of all three ships were told to stay in their cabins, and the men went to work.

Many of these men had guarded the ships, so they knew their layout well. Many, too, worked on the docks and knew how to load and unload vessels quickly and efficiently. On each ship the men formed three teams. One went below the deck to bring out the chests; others worked the hoists and tackles to bring the chests up from the hold; others split the chests with their hatchets and dumped them over the side. "Perfect regularity prevailed during the whole transaction," one observer noted. "Although there were many people on the wharf, entire silence prevailed,—no clamor, no talking." Each squad captain kept careful tally against the manifest, ensuring that every chest of East India Company tea, and only the East India Company's tea, was destroyed.

Captain Coffin asked the men not to start with the *Beaver,* as he had cargo stowed on top of the tea. Coffin feared damage to these less controversial goods. The men told him that it was "the tea they wanted, and the tea they would have"; they sent Coffin to his cabin and then unloaded his cargo onto the dock before turning their attention to the tea.

Tide was out. The piles of broken chests and mounds of tea formed islands in the shallow water. Apprentices and boys were sent over the sides of the ships to break up the mountains of chests and scatter the hills of tea. As these men worked, others saw an opportunity. A few small boats appeared in the shallow water, rowing toward the islands of tea. Armed men on the dock warned the boats away, swearing to "shoot any Person that offered to touch the Tea." A man named Connor, or O'Connor, an Irish horse dealer, found the temptation too much. He cut the seams of his pockets and tried to fill his coat lining with the fragrant tea. George Robert Twelves Hewes spotted Connor, whom he knew, seized his coat, and tore it off. Connor escaped, without coat or tea, through a gauntlet of spectators who beat him and pelted him with harbor mud. The next day his torn coat was displayed, nailed to the Charlestown whipping post.

By ten o'clock the three ships had been unloaded: 342 chests, 92,586 pounds of East India Company tea valued at £9,659 (approximately $1,738,500 today), spread over the flats of Boston Harbor, waiting for the tide to take it away.

Their work done, the men closed the holds, stowed the tackle, swept the decks, and invited the officers up to inspect the work. One of the squads had broken a padlock—a scout went to find a replacement. The keys were returned, the manifests were checked, and the men set out for home.

THE IMMEDIATE WORK of destroying the tea was done. But what would come next? First, there was a sense of jubilation in town. "Those persons who were from the Country, returned with a merry Heart," the *Boston News-Letter* reported, "and the next Day Joy appeared in almost every countenance," some because of "the destruction of the Tea, others on Account of the Quietness with which it was effected." Even Captains Hall, Bruce, and Coffin and the shipowners Francis Rotch and John Rowe were "well pleased that their Ships are thus cleared" and ready to load a return cargo. Meanwhile, the shore from Boston's south end docks all around to Dorchester Neck was littered with broken chests and salty tea.

"This is the most magnificent Movement of all," John Adams wrote in his diary. "There is a Dignity, a Majesty, a Sublimity, in this last Effort of the Patriots, that I greatly admire." In defending the soldiers respon-

*This 1784 German engraving has the wrong date, but it does show an Indian and an African American watching the destruction. (Courtesy Library of Congress)*

Die Einwohner von Boston werfen den englisch-oftindischen Thee ins Meer am 18. December 1773.

sible for the Boston Massacre, Adams had put the Boston mob on trial and found them guilty. Now, in this act of protest, he saw a majesty and sublimity absent on March 5, 1770. "The People should never rise, without doing something to be remembered—something notable And striking. This Destruction of the Tea is so bold, so daring, so firm, intrepid and inflexible, and it must have so important Consequences, and so lasting, that I cant but consider it as an Epocha in History."

Was it necessary to destroy the tea? Adams wrote that it was "absolutely and indispensably" necessary. Governor Hutchinson, Admiral Montagu, the customs officials could have saved it by allowing it to return to England. But they refused. The only alternatives then were to destroy it or land it. "To let it be landed, would be giving up the Principle of Taxation by Parliamentary Authority, against which the Continent have struggled for 10 years," Adams continued. It would mean giving up this decade-long fight and submitting "ourselves and our Posterity forever to Egyptian Taskmasters—to Burthens, Indignities, to Ignominy, Reproach and Contempt, to Desolation and oppression, to Poverty and Servitude."

Adams placed the blame for the episode on Hutchinson, the inflexible Governor, and on the consignees. They had "stood and looked upon the distresses of the People, and their Struggles to get the Tea back to London," unmoved in their "hardened and abandoned" hearts. Visitors came to see Adams and reported that the Tories also blamed the consignees for the destruction, and predicted that "the Governor will loose his Place" for failing to protect the tea. Isaiah Thomas's *Massachusetts Spy* reported that the consignees' "obstinacy has rendered them infinitely more obnoxious to their countrymen than even the Stamp-Masters were," and it predicted that "their names will be transmitted to posterity with ten fold infamy." An anonymous writer reported in the *Spy* that, "having sold their country," the consignees were "purchasing a number of negroes, and preparing to embark for the Bay of Honduras, as they fear no other part of the world will receive them." Anne Hulton, a sister of Customs Commissioner Henry Hulton, wrote that "all the Malice that the Earth & Hell could raise were pointed against the Governor."

Calling it "the boldest stroke that had been struck in America," Hutchinson tried to take action against the perpetrators. He went into Boston, passing Adams's window in his carriage, and summoned the Governor's Council to a meeting at the State House. But a quorum of the council did not appear, and though Hutchinson vowed to have the those responsible tried and found "guilty of High Treason," he could not act. John Hancock remarked coolly that he would call a meeting of the body of the people "to take off that Brother in Law of his," Peter Oliver.

Hutchinson left Boston for Castle Island, calling for another council meeting the next day, Saturday, December 18, at his home in Milton. Still there was no quorum, and Hutchinson could not meet with his council until Tuesday, when it convened at the Cambridge home of William Brattle. Hutchinson wanted the council to offer a reward for the apprehension of those responsible; instead, the council advised that the attorney general investigate and if necessary take his findings to a grand jury.

While Hutchinson was desperately and futilely trying to bring down the law on the perpetrators, the committees of correspondence were equally busy, and more successful, in spreading their version of the events. As Hutchinson was trying to convene his council on Friday, Paul Revere was on his way to New York; by the time Hutchinson finally convened a quorum the following Tuesday, December 21, Revere had already delivered the report of Boston's decisive action. On that day, New Yorkers read that "The Moment it was known out of Doors, that Mr. Rotch could not obtain a Pass for his Ship," a number of people "huzza'd in the Street, and in a very little Time, every Ounce of the Teas on board . . . was immersed in the Bay, without the least Injury to private Property."

Another rider set off from New York for Philadelphia. At five o'clock in the afternoon on Friday, December 24, Christmas Eve, the *Pennsylvania Journal* published a special "Christmas-Box," for its customers, carrying the account of Boston's decisive action.

The next night the *Polly* reached Chester, south of Philadelphia. On the morning after Christmas a committee from Philadelphia went to meet Gilbert Barkley, a consignee who had come from England on the ship. After Barkley was told that the "sentiments of the city" were that his cargo endangered "the public liberties of America," he resigned his commission.

Meanwhile, the *Polly* made its way up the Delaware River, until a committee hailed it at Gloucester Point. Captain Ayres stopped the ship and came ashore. The committee escorted him to the public meeting called for the State House. On an hour's notice eight thousand Philadelphians had gathered, and they crowded into the open square in front of the State House. Ayres was persuaded to return to England. Philadelphia merchants expecting shipments of goods aboard the *Polly* agreed to let them all go back to England with the ship. They shuttled provisions down to Gloucester Point for the *Polly*'s return voyage, and a great crowd accompanied Ayres and Barkley back to the river, where they "wished them a good voyage" and put them on a pilot boat to go downriver. The *Polly* sailed for England, and the Philadelphia meeting adjourned, giving "their hearty thanks to the people at Boston for their resolution in destroying the tea rather than suffer it to be landed."

REVERE RETURNED TO BOSTON on Monday, December 27. News of New York's reception "gave great satisfaction to all the friends of liberty." Governor Tryon had vowed to land the tea, but he relented when he learned that Bostonians had destroyed the three cargoes. He would not have the East India Company's tea destroyed in New York. When the *Nancy* arrived, he would allow the ship to take on provisions so it could return with its cargo to England. The tea would not be unloaded in New York. Every church bell in Boston rang out at this news. Bostonians could not force Hutchinson to back down, but their bold action had forced Governor Tryon to concede. In a related development, John Vardill, the anonymous author of the Poplicola essays, returned to England.

With this affirmation from New York, the New Englanders continued to press their cause. On Christmas day a Newport, Rhode Island, Patriot wrote to a friend in Boston, "I most heartily rejoice at the glorious stroke given to tyranny by the noble Bostonians in the destruction of the India company's tea, and can assure you, if any comes here, which is doubtful, it will meet with a similar fate."

CHAPTER FIVE

# The Political
# Aftermath at Home

BOSTON'S PRINCIPAL TEA DEALERS—except for the consignees—met on December 20 and again on Thursday, December 23, one week after the destruction of the tea. They voted not to sell any more tea after January 20, 1774, and not to purchase tea from any source before that time. Tea then on hand could be sold for no more than a four-pence profit. Charlestown's Town Meeting on Tuesday, December 28, appointed a committee to collect all the tea in town. Pledging not to "buy or sell" tea, or to allow any tea to be sold until Parliament repealed the revenue acts, Charlestown appointed a Committee of Inspection to oversee the collection and destruction of all the tea in town. Calling anyone who hindered the Town's action an enemy "to the Liberty of America in general" and guilty of "disrespect to this Town in particular," Charlestown called on other towns to follow them in banning the use of tea.

To make a dramatic point, on December 30 Charlestown's Committee of Inspection piled all its confiscated tea in the town marketplace. A thousand people gathered at noon, enjoying punch and wine provided by Charlestown's Sons of Liberty. "The Charlestown sons treated the Boston people very gentley," wrote a Bostonian, Thomas Newell. All enjoyed the warmth and spectacle of the bonfire that destroyed Charlestown's confiscated tea.

The next evening a Dorchester committee called on the Withington brothers, Ebenezer and Philip, at their homes on the road

*One of the few chests that survived the axe and the bonfire; its cover was removed by hatchet, and its wood shows signs of having been in salt water. It was recovered the morning after the tea's destruction from the Dorchester marshes, and it will be displayed at the Boston Tea Party Museum. (Courtesy Boston Tea Party Museum)*

to Milton. Rumor had it that that Ebenezer Withington had gathered tea off the marshes between Dorchester Neck and Boston. The Withingtons consented to have their homes searched, but no tea was found. The committee then visited another Ebenezer Withington, "Old Ebenezer Withington," who lived "at a Place called Sodom, below Dorchester Meeting House." They found half a chest of tea in his house, took it to Boston, and shortly before midnight on New Year's Eve burned it on Boston Common.

Withington appeared three days later at the Dorchester Town Meeting to apologize. "I found said Tea on Saturday, on going round upon the Marshes," he explained, and, "thinking no harm," he had taken it home. On the way home, he had met some men from Castle Island, who asked if he was "picking up the Ruins," and Withington asked what harm there was in it. There would be no harm, they said, "except from [his] neighbors."

Some neighbors bought tea from Withington, others reported him. The Town Meeting resolved that Withington had acted out of "inadvertency" and was pleased that he had been discovered—"otherwise the Conspirators against our Rights and Liberties" would have claimed that Bostonians had not destroyed the tea, but had stolen it and sold it for private gain.

While this stray tea was being confiscated and burned, Jonathan Clarke left Castle Island for Provincetown to gather up the tea wrecked on the *William*. Just as the Bostonians "thou't themselves at Liberty to destroy what Tea was there," Clarke feared the people of Provincetown might "think themselves licensed to steal what is here." Clarke and John Greenough, the Wellfleet justice of the peace, secured what remained of the cargo, and Clarke tried to charter a vessel to take it to Boston. Two Boston captains refused to carry the tea, but John Cook of Salem agreed to take it to Castle Island.

Cook unloaded the tea at Castle Island, though it was said the "Tea Consignees had better have had a mill-stone tied around their necks" than have the tea at the Castle, as the fort on Castle Island was known. That evening when Cook docked in Boston, "a number of Indians" searched his ship, but they found no tea. Cook quickly sailed home to Salem. The ship's owner, George Bickford, checked himself into the Essex hospital to be inoculated for smallpox, though rumors spread that this was a ploy to avoid punishment for allowing his sloop to carry the tea. Certain he was not carrying smallpox, "a company of natives, dressed in the Indian manner, armed with hatchets, axes, &c.," visited the hospital. But when they discovered he actually had smallpox, they "deferred proceeding to extremities."

In Plymouth thirteen of the forty protestors recanted on December 30, and the next day a meeting was called to deal with the other twenty-seven. At three o'clock in the afternoon on New Year's Eve, an assembly of townspeople gathered in the courthouse to discuss the recalcitrant protestors. Two of the protestors, Thomas Foster and Pelham Winslow, came to the meeting in their position as town magistrates, and they declared it an illegal gathering. But unlike Greenleaf, who had ordered the Boston meeting to disperse, Foster and Winslow told their fellow townspeople that if they had business, they should have the selectmen issue a warrant for a meeting. If the selectmen refused a warrant, Winslow and Foster promised to issue one.

The people in the meeting agreed to this proposal, but before dispersing they read a letter that another of the protestors, Colonel George Watson, Elisha Hutchinson's father-in-law, had received that morning from Boston. The writer promised to tar and feather Watson if he ever visited Boston. Although the meeting had assembled to deal with protestors like Watson, Boston's threat to tar and feather him stirred resentment in Plymouth. If the writer of the letter had been at the Plymouth meeting, "he must have felt the severe Effects of their Resentment." News also reached Plymouth that another of their protestors, Barnabas Hedge, had been treated roughly in Boston. This intimidation and violence had lessened "the Number of the Sons of Liberty" in Plymouth, where many people had the opinion "that every one should enjoy their own Sentiments, and make them public without Reserve."

The actions of some Bostonians annoyed other communities. Charlestown's Sons of Liberty were incensed when some Boston merchants, "esteemed friends to liberty," tried to send a barrel of tea out to the country for sale; having destroyed the tea in their community, they did not want to allow Boston merchants to ship their tea. They seized the barrel and emptied its contents into the Charles River.

THE BOSTON SONS OF LIBERTY moved to prevent further sale of tea. After the tea dealers had met in December and voted not to sell any tea after January 20, a committee of dealers had called on all the merchants in town to sign the no-tea pledge. Seventy-nine merchants had signed; nine others had said they would sell only tea that was not subject to the tax. "It is wished," the *Massachusetts Spy* wrote, "that the few who have not" signed the agreement "will, on a reconsideration, perceive the utility and necessity of the measure, and immediately join their disinterested fellow citizens in the same resolutions." On January 20, as a signal of their resolution not to allow any tea to be sold, the committee had a bonfire on King Street and destroyed three barrels, about seven hundred pounds, of bohea tea.

As this campaign against smuggled, non-taxed tea was beginning, the campaign against the consignees was still raging. A notice plastered throughout Boston warned that the tea consignees—"those odious Miscreants and detestable tools to Ministry and Governor," who were also "Traitors to their Country, Butchers," and were doing all in their power "to murder and destroy" all who stood in the way of their private interest—were planning to move back to town. Bostonians were urged to give them the kind of reception "such vile Ingrates" deserved. It was signed Joyce, Junior, "Chairman of the Committee for Tarring and Feathering." Joyce was the name of the Cromwell supporter who had captured King Charles I in 1647; the Bostonian Joyce, Junior, was known for his clear and loud whistle, which could summon or control a crowd, and was seen leading various crowds in his red coat and white wig.

The tea consignees did not return to Boston. It was reported in mid-January that one of them had slipped into town and only narrowly escaped tarring and feathering. "Presumptuous men," the paper said, "to think of gaining a footing in this town again." Another report from Milton said that "a certain great Man in that town," presumably Governor Hutchinson, heard a gun in the distance and immediately "ran trembling into his castle." Without a trace of sympathy, it was concluded, "A miserable life this!—Always in fear and horror!"

Elisha Hutchinson and his wife, Mary, slipped down to Plymouth on January 17 to visit his father-in-law. Knowing of the active opposition to the protests in Plymouth, Hutchinson expected less trouble than in Boston. But when news spread that he was in town, the church bells tolled and a "great appearance" of people assembled at Colonel Watson's house. They demanded Hutchinson's "instant departure from the town." Members of the Committee of Correspondence interceded—it was late at night, and they would allow Hutchinson to spend the night. The next morning a snowstorm blew up, and the Hutchinsons delayed their departure—"either over-sleeping," the paper reported, or Elisha wanted to test "the tempers of the people"—but the crowd gathered in front of the house and forced the Hutchinsons to leave. They made their way in the storm to the Middleborough home of Mary Hutchinson's grandfather Peter Oliver.

In Boston rumors that Ebenezer Richardson had returned were circulating. Richardson, hated for his role as a customs informant in the late 1760s and convicted of killing Christopher Seider in 1770, had been at large since Governor Hutchinson arranged a pardon and had him spirited out of town. The hunt for Richardson consumed many, but while he proved elusive, a more visible target appeared in the person of John Malcolm. Malcolm had served under Governor Tryon in the suppression of the Regulators of North Carolina; since then he had been in New England and had informed the customs officials in Maine about a vessel with an unregistered cargo. The officials had seized the vessel, but a crowd of sailors had "genteely tarr'd and feather'd" Malcolm, leaving his clothes on as they did the deed.

Malcolm came to Boston, where he let people know his feelings, making "free and open declarations against the late proceedings" on the tea. He complained to Hutchinson of "being hooted at in the streets for having been tarred and feathered." Hutchinson thought Malcolm might have "indiscreetly provoked" the populace. Hoping to keep things calm, Hutchinson cautioned Malcolm, a "passionate man," not to respond to these taunts. But on January 25 a boy in Boston pushed Malcolm too far. George Robert Twelves Hewes came upon Malcolm on Fore Street standing over the boy, "cursing, damning, threatening, and shaking a very large cane with a very heavy ferril on it over his head." According to the account in the *Boston Gazette,* as Malcolm brandished his club over the boy, Hewes stepped in.

"Mr. Malcolm, I hope you are not going to strike this boy with that stick."

Calling Hewes an "impertinent rascal," Malcolm told him it was none of his business. Hewes asked what the boy had done. Malcolm damned Hewes for taking the boy's side. Hewes told him he thought it a shame that Malcolm would hit the boy with such a dangerous weapon. Malcolm again damned Hewes, calling him a vagabond who should not talk to gentlemen in the street. Hewes insisted that though he was poor, he was as good as Malcolm. Malcolm called Hewes a liar, and Hewes said, "Be that as it will, I never was tarred and feathered anyhow."

This sent Malcolm over the edge, and he brought down his cane over Hewes's head, practically breaking his skull. Dazed and nearly fainting, Hewes made his way to Dr. Joseph Warren and then to a magistrate to swear out a complaint against Malcolm. A crowd now chased

Malcolm, who barricaded himself in his house, where the crowd jeered him for having been tarred and feathered. "Damn you," Malcolm shouted back, "let me see the man that dare do it better."

The crowd determined to oblige him. That evening a mob arrived at his house and broke his windows. They became furious when Malcolm cut some of the attackers with a sword he brandished through the broken panes. Leaders of the Sons of Liberty arrived, and they urged the crowd not to attack Malcolm but to seek justice through the courts. The angry crowd asked what justice the law had meted out to Richardson, or to Captain Thomas Preston and soldiers involved in the Boston Massacre.

They wrested Malcolm from his home, stripped him to his under-clothes, and "gave him a modern jacket" of tar and feathers. More than a thousand people accompanied the procession to the Liberty Tree, where they demanded that Malcolm renounce his commission and swear not to take another post "inconsistent with the liberties of his country." He refused, shouting defiantly, "Curse all Traitors." They took him to the gallows on the Common, tied a noose around his neck, and threw the other end over the beam, then beat him with the rope's end, threatening to cut off his ears. While some pleaded with a justice of the peace "to Exert his Authority & suppress" the violence, promising to "support him in the execution of his Duty," the judge refused. Finally, the threat of imminent death at the hands of this crowd persuaded Malcolm to resign his commission, and he was taken home "terribly bruised" but likely to recover.

Anne Hulton, the sister of the customs commissioner, saw the government of Massachusetts unraveling, as the mob was not trying simply to punish Malcolm, but to intimidate the judges of the province. "There's no Majestrate that dare or will act to suppress the outrages," she wrote. The next night a mob turned out to look for Richardson.

Joyce, Junior, posted another notice at the end of January, certifying "that the modern Punishment lately inflicted on the ignoble JOHN MALCOLM, was not done by our Order." Still signing himself "Chairman of the Committee for Tarring and Feathering," Joyce, Junior, reserved tar and feathers for "Villains of greater Consequence."

Hutchinson opened a session of the Massachusetts Assembly on January 26. He wrote to the Earl of Dartmouth that he "endeavoured

*This British cartoon shows the Bostonians tarring and feathering John Malcolm at the Liberty Tree, in January 1774; behind them is the destruction of the tea. (Courtesy Library of Congress)*

to make such a speech to them as should show I had no inclination to dispute with them upon any point whatsoever." He told the assembly there had never been a time "since the first settlement of the country when the Treasury has been in so good a state as it is now." They were free from debt and their taxes covered all the charges, though Hutchinson suggested a "moderate duty" on liquor to offset the need for any borrowing. He told the assembly that they needed to act on the claim the Indians of Martha's Vineyard had made to Chappaquiddick Island, as the Indians had petitioned the king, who wanted a just resolution. Hutchinson was also able to tell the assembly that the king would approve the boundary settlement he had negotiated with New York, ending this "source of so much mischief" between the two colonies. In the midst of this positive news, Hutchinson was "required to signify to you his Majesty's disapprobation of the appointment of Committees of correspondence in various instances, which sit and act during the recess of the General Court." Except for this one negative note, Hutchinson avoided all talk of the recent calamitous events, though he called on the assembly to promote the "tranquility and good order of the government." He told Dartmouth that if he had "enlarged upon the late disorder," the assembly would have adopted the "substance of what I lately received from the Council and probably would have charged me with forcing such an answer from them."

The assembly, though, would not be placated. The previous year the British ministry had proposed having the Crown pay the judges in the American colonies. The purpose was to ensure that those judges would not be subject to political pressure and thus could make unbiased decisions. Part of the impetus was the Boston Massacre of 1770, after which British soldiers had been tried in an American court. Though the soldiers were found not guilty, there was still a fear that American courts would not always be neutral. Having the judges depend for their salaries on the British Crown, rather than the provincial assemblies, would help ensure judicial independence.

But the Massachusetts Assembly listened to Samuel Adams's call to heed the provincial charter of 1691, which gave the assembly the power to pay the judges. The assembly had demanded that all judges renounce the Crown's salary. All judges of the superior court had done so, except for Chief Justice Peter Oliver. Now, in February 1774, the assembly moved to impeach Oliver. Governor Hutchinson thought this an affront to the king that it would "leave a lasting stain upon the character of the government."

As this constitutional drama was beginning, the ship *Fortune* reached Boston carrying twenty-eight chests of tea. This tea belonged not to the East India Company but to private merchants. Still, on the night of March 8, 1774, members "of Oknookortunkogog tribe" boarded the *Fortune* and dumped the tea overboard. Hutchinson wrote that the tea's owners "are very silent, and I think if they could find out who were the immediate actors they would not venture at present to bring any action in the law against them." They did not want to share the fate of Hutchinson's sons and the Clarkes, the other consignees.

The same day as this second Boston tea party, Hutchinson's brother-in-law, Lieutenant Governor Andrew Oliver, who died on March 3 under strain from the political turmoil, was buried. Though the funeral was well attended, neither the council nor most of the House of Representatives attended, and on their way home Oliver's relatives, presumably including the governor, met with "Some Rude Behaviour." Hutchinson terminated the assembly.

CHAPTER SIX

# The Empire
# Strikes Back

WHILE HUTCHINSON WAS TRYING to keep peace in Massachusetts, news reached England of the destruction of the tea. Hancock's ship, *Hayley,* reached London on January 20. Two days later London's papers carried the *Boston Gazette's* account of the tea's destruction, and as Hutchinson was opening the Massachusetts Assembly on January 26, the *Polly* reached England with the tea it could not unload in Philadelphia.

Benjamin Franklin, representing the Massachusetts Assembly in London, had arranged for the Privy Council to hear the assembly's charges against Hutchinson and Lieutenant Governor Andrew Oliver. Unfortunately for Franklin, the hearing was scheduled for January 29, just as London was learning all the details of the tea's destruction. The Privy Council was in no mood to hear the grievances of Massachusetts. Solicitor General Alexander Wedderburn turned the hearing into a vicious attack on Franklin, blaming him for stirring up anger against Hutchinson by sending the Whately correspondence to Boston. Those letters, written by Hutchinson in the 1760s, had stirred the assembly's wrath against Hutchinson in the early summer of 1773. Thereafter, Wedderburn charged, Franklin would cringe at being called a "man of letters." In fact, Wedderburn continued, Franklin was little more than a common thief, with an exaggerated sense of his own importance and an inflated sense of his station. Instead of being a representative from a provincial assembly, Franklin imagined himself to be the ambassador of an independent empire! The packed hearing room enjoyed the public humiliation of Benjamin Franklin, who was summarily dismissed as the deputy postmaster for the American colonies.

That same day Lord North met with the rest of the cabinet to work out a new policy that would "secure the Dependance of the Colonies on the Mother Country." On February 5 the Earl of Dartmouth submitted his report to the attorney general and the solicitor general, outlining what had happened in Boston, identifying the ringleaders in the attacks on the Clarkes and in the various meetings, and asking if these actions constituted high treason. One week later Dartmouth received his answer. Those responsible—Molineux, Warren, Church, and others who had attacked Clarke, and Williams, Samuel Adams, Dr. Young, and John Hancock, ringleaders in the November 28 and 30 meetings—were all guilty of high treason. If these men were acting on behalf of the Town of Boston or Province of Massachusetts, then the selectmen, town clerk, and provincial assembly were also guilty.

They could either be tried in America or transported to England. The legal minds thought the "more ordinary course," having them tried in America, would be preferable.

ON MAY 10 NEWS REACHED BOSTON that effective June 1, the harbor was closed. The customhouse would move to Salem, and no ship could unload its cargo in Boston, at least until Boston paid the company for the tea it had destroyed. Three days later General Thomas Gage arrived to be the new governor of Massachusetts. The assembly had pushed to have Hutchinson replaced, and he would be—by the commander of all British military forces in North America. The merchant John Rowe hoped that Gage's "Instructions be not severe as I think him to be a Very Good Man." But by replacing Hutchinson, a mild-mannered but firm son of Massachusetts, with Gage, a military officer, Parliament and the British ministry were signaling that they were not going to tolerate any more disorder in Massachusetts. Gage spent a few days at Castle Island before formally arriving in town on May 17. Gage spoke to the Massachusetts Assembly, telling it that on June 1 he would meet with its members in Salem, where the government of the province would thenceforth sit.

*The able Doctor, or America Swallowing the Bitter Draught.*

*This British cartoon shows Lord North, with the Boston Port Bill in his pocket, forcing tea down America's throat as other British officials hold her down and look up her dress. (Courtesy Library of Congress)*

Meanwhile, Boston's town committee—Samuel and John Adams, Josiah Quincy, William Phillips, Henderson Inches, William Molineux, Thomas Cushing, and John Rowe—met to decide how to respond to the closing of the port. The Town called for a general meeting of delegates from all the colonies—a continental congress—to come up with a unified plan. The Town dispatched Paul Revere with the call. Would the colonies side with Boston? Or would each colony follow its own best interest in placating the British Empire?

The destruction of the tea had precipitated this crisis. Had the *Polly*, bound for Philadelphia, been the first tea ship to arrive in America, the situation would have been different. There the consignees had resigned, and the governor, answerable to the Penn family, not the British Crown, had taken no role in the crisis. The tea would have returned to England undamaged. Though the North ministry would have been angry and determined to prove its point, it would not have had justification for military force.

Had the *Nancy* reached New York in October or November 1773, rather than April 1774, the issue too would have been different. There, though the consignees had resigned, Governor Tryon was determined to land the tea, and it is doubtful the Sons of Liberty could have prevented it. There would have been protests and agitation, but the East India Company, at least in the short term, might have prevailed. But the same storm that wrecked the *William* had battered the *Nancy,* which spent much of the winter being repaired in Antigua. Though the *Nancy's* Captain Lockyer learned about Boston's reaction to the tea, he was still determined to sail to New York. Perhaps he expected that the consignees would have pressed Governor Tryon and the British ministry to do more to ensure their cargo's safety; instead, he found a town determined to resist. He anchored off Sandy Hook on April 18 and went into New York to discuss options with the consignees. New York's Sons of Liberty met him at the dock. He and the consignees agreed to return the tea to England. As it had in Philadelphia, news of the tea's departure set off celebrations in New York.

In May two ships carrying tea reached the Chesapeake. The reaction was so extreme when one of Anthony Stewart's ships, the *Peggy Stewart,* brought a ton of tea into Annapolis, that Stewart, to placate the crowd and prevent their destruction of all his other holdings, had the ship set on fire with the tea in it—to the great joy of all onlookers. When a tea ship reached Chestertown, a party of men, not even bothering with disguises, boarded a vessel in broad daylight and dumped the tea into the Chesapeake. Boston had made the case plain—the tea had to be destroyed.

Had the tea landed first in Maryland, New York, Philadelphia, or Charleston, South Carolina, the reaction would have been much different. But instead the tea ships sailed into Boston, into a simmering conflict between Governor Hutchinson and the Massachusetts Assembly, and between the Clarkes and Hutchinsons and other tea merchants and Hancock and his allies. Boston's active and mobilized Sons of Liberty were prepared at a moment's notice to take to the streets to avenge insults to their dignity or their affronted liberty.

"Poor unhappy Boston," John Rowe wrote in his diary on June 1, the day the port was shut. "God knows only thy wretched fate. I see nothing but misery will attend thy inhabitants."

ON MAY 31, THE LAST DAY VESSELS could legally sail out of Boston, Thomas Hutchinson, "that bad governor," as Thomas Newell, a tinsmith, called him, sailed for England with his daughter Peggy and his son Elisha. Now the only arrivals into the harbor would be troopships. On June 2 news arrived that the charter of 1691 was suspended; the government of Massachusetts now would be in the hands of Gage, who would appoint all local magistrates and sheriffs. Town meetings could assemble only once a year, and then only with the governor's consent. The assembly met and chose delegates to a general congress of the American colonies, but as they were meeting and choosing Hancock, James Bowdoin, Robert Treat Paine, and Samuel and John Adams, the governor's secretary was nailing a proclamation to their door dissolving the assembly.

Now the only activity in the harbor would be the arrival of more warships. The port was closed, "by the cruel edict of the British Parliament." Invoking the lament of David on the defeat of Israel and the death of King Saul at the hands of the Philistines, "How are the mighty fallen? Tell it not in Gath, publish it not in the streets of Askelon" (a reference to two Philistine cities), Thomas Newell closed his account of the British suppression of Boston, "Tell it in Gath, publish it in Askelon."

John Adams had been chosen as a delegate to the Continental Congress, which would meet in Philadelphia in September. Before he set off in August for his first trip out of Massachusetts, he spent the summer riding the circuit, arguing cases for clients in the courts of Maine (still part of Massachusetts). He did not dare to hope that the Congress would stand with Massachusetts in its cause against Parliament. In the meantime, he had to work as a lawyer to earn a living for his wife and four children in Braintree (now Quincy, Massachusetts). After a thirty-five-mile ride on a hot July afternoon, Adams arrived at Falmouth (now Portland, Maine). Weary, dusty, and hot, Adams hoped to relax and revive with a cup of his favorite beverage. "Madam," he asked Mrs. Huston, "is it lawfull for a weary Traveller to refresh himself with a Dish of Tea provided it has been honestly smuggled, or paid no Duties?"

"No sir, we have renounced all Tea in this Place." Mrs. Huston's patriotism far exceeded his own, he found. "I can't make tea," she said, but, pointing to her husband, offered, "but He make you coffee."

*This British print mocks the fifty-one ladies of Edenton, North Carolina, who pledged not to drink tea in October 1774. (Courtesy Library of Congress)*

For the rest of his time in Falmouth, Adams "drank Coffee every Afternoon" and bore it well. He discovered that the people of New England had taken heart from Boston's destruction of the tea. Before 1773 upwardly mobile Americans had adopted tea as a social beverage; now Americans renounced tea as a patriotic duty. The East India consignees had been driven out of town; the smugglers found the American market for tea had disappeared. "Tea must be universally renounced," Adams said. "I must be weaned, and the sooner, the better."

THE DESTRUCTION OF THE TEA brought on the American Revolution. In reaction, Parliament closed the port of Boston and suspended the government of Massachusetts, replacing the government of the charter with government by force of British arms. But the problem was not simply Boston; the work of the committees of correspondence had spread resistance to every colony. When the Continental Congress assembled in Philadelphia, though it hoped for reconciliation, it also was firm in resisting Parliament's attempts either to tax the colonists or to force East India tea upon them. In April 1775, knowing that citizens in the towns of Massachusetts were stockpiling weapons for resistance in Lexington and Concord, Governor Gage ordered his troops out to destroy the caches. The British troops succeeded, but they encountered armed resistance, and militia troops—ordinary citizens who took up arms for the defense of their communities—attacked the retreating British regulars on the road back to Boston. By the end of the day, Gage and his armies were besieged in Boston; the rest of the province was in the hands of people in rebellion against his authority.

The Congress, still in Philadelphia, vowed continued resistance. On May 10, 1776, three years after Parliament passed the Tea Act, two years after Gage had arrived in Massachusetts, the Congress called on the American colonies to draw up new governments, and on July 4, 1776, it declared that these thirteen colonies were, and of right should be, free and independent states, the United States of America.

Long after the fact, in the 1830s, the events of December 16, 1773, would be called the Boston Tea Party. At the time, all were aware of the seriousness of what was occurring. They knew they were committing high treason against the empire. But in doing so they were performing a patriotic duty toward the land that was their country. The events of that night shook the empire and began the war for independence. It was a bold move and, as John Adams noted, an "epocha" in history. It was a rising of the people—and a rising in Boston that sparked a unification of the American colonies.

By resisting the East India Company's tea, the American colonies avoided the fate of Bengal. But the East India Company expanded its hold on India. Lord Cornwallis, who surrendered to the American forces at Yorktown in 1781, later served as governor general of India, and by the early nineteenth century the British had subjugated all of India's provinces and kingdoms. The British suppressed rebellions in India through military force, convincing the colonized people of the country that they could not resist the arms of the empire. After two wars about England's right to introduce opium into China, the British flag also flew over Hong Kong. Though they had lost their North American colonies, the British could still proudly say that the sun never set on their empire.

India produced cotton for the British textile industry, which bought it cheaply and sold it back more dearly as manufactured cloth. In 1930 the British government in India placed a tax on salt. Traditionally, the people of India would harvest salt on the hot beaches of the Indian Ocean, using this necessity to preserve fish. Now the British government would require the people of India to purchase salt, which was essential for their diet, and to pay a tax for this privilege. A sixty-one-year-old Indian lawyer trained in London, Mohandas K. Gandhi, led a twenty-three-day march of Indian people to the beach at Dandi. Gandhi knew that Indians had become dependent on British manufactured goods, and he had resisted this dependence by weaving his own cloth. He had given up the tailored suit of a British lawyer and now dressed simply in a homespun loincloth. And he absolutely re-jected the use of violence in resisting British rule. Crowds gathered and joined Gandhi and his small group of followers on their 240-mile march to Dandi. Along the route he spoke of the possibilities of inde-pendence. He awakened the people of India to their own power. On the beach at Dandi, Gandhi gathered salt.

Like the Boston Tea Party, the Salt March shook the British Empire. Gandhi was imprisoned, but he had aroused a force the British government could not ignore. Protests throughout India threatened the British grip, and finally the British viceroy, Lord Irwin, agreed to release Gandhi. Irwin even summoned Gandhi to meet with him.

At the viceroy's palace, Lord Irwin offered Gandhi tea. Would Mr. Gandhi take cream or sugar in his tea? No, Gandhi replied. But he would like to flavor his tea with salt, as a reminder of others who had resisted Britain's arbitrary rule.

# BIBLIOGRAPHICAL NOTE

BENJAMIN WOOD LABAREE'S *The Boston Tea Party* (New York: Oxford University Press, 1964; available in paperback in a Northeastern Classics Edition, 1979) is the standard work on the events of December 16, 1773, as well as on the background to the Tea Act. Alfred Young's *The Shoemaker and the Tea Party* (Boston: Beacon Press, 1999) tells the story of George Robert Twelves Hewes, a participant in the event, and explores the way the Tea Party has been recalled in the popular memory. Francis Samuel Drake's *Tea Leaves* (Boston: A. O. Crane, 1884) republishes transcripts and minutes of most of the public meetings preceding the arrival of the tea, as well as commentary on its destruction.

The Massachusetts Historical Society, in addition to the papers of John Adams available online (www.masshist.org), has the diaries of Thomas Newell and John Rowe and other miscellaneous letters and documents pertinent to the story. I am indebted to Peter Drummey and to Carolle Morini for their help uncovering these sources. The Boston Public Library has a terrific collection of newspapers, many available on their Web site (www.bpl.org), and I thank especially Marta Pardee-King for assisting with these.

The Bostonian Society has a strong collections of images of Boston, and I thank Cindy Mackey and Rainey Tisdale for their assistance. Historic Tours of America, which operates the Boston Tea Party Museum, has been helpful with imagery and enthusiasm for the story. I thank especially Dana Ste. Claire and Lana Gantner for their assistance.

# INDEX

*Page references given in italics indicate illustrations or material contained in their captions.*

.